Straight from the Pen:
Writing Wrongs

edited by:

LORI B. SUTTON

Adjunct faculty, San Diego State University

&

L. PAUL SUTTON, PhD

Professor Emeritus, Criminal Justice Program
School of Public Affairs, San Diego State University

foreword by John E. Brown, *writer, teacher*
Wichita, Kansas

JustUs Educational Partners
psutton@mail.sdsu.edu
https://sites.google.com/site/justuseducationalpartners/

Published by: JustUs Educational Partners; c/o L. Paul Sutton
Location: El Cajon, CA 92019-4554
Website: https://sites.google.com/site/justuseducationalpartners/
Cover design: L. Paul Sutton
Cover art: Roberta F. Sutton
Interior art: by the writers in our RJD classes

First published 2017

Manufactured in the United States

ISBN-10: 0692930205
ISBN-13: 978-0692930205

Library of Congress CIP data applied for

TABLE OF CONTENTS

FOREWORD
John E. Brown

Microsoft Word be damned, far as I'm concerned. I believe that the movement of the human arm, the human hand, across a clean sheet of white paper gives forth thought. I think ideas flow from the hand-written word as surely as does a creek from a mountain storm.

I said to them, "Write it for a reason." I asked these men, subject to the unreasonable for most of their days and ways, to for once think about logical consequence. About what might happen based on a choice in the here and now. About how the selection of a concrete, specific noun operating through a strong, active verb might grab the wind, might shove the mind off to a tight kernel of thought, might say exactly what a man might mean. Three rules here: tell the truth; be respectful; have fun, the last of these terms not once a waste among men longing to laugh.

I found them easy to love.

Smart, attentive, open to a joke, wanting in the sweat and fear of a public moment to put thought right, to channel the power of a language with a half-million, non-technical words, but theirs the language of the second-grader, right and good for them and for me— the single-syllable Anglo-Saxon heart of an English alive to us, bright now in the sight of all that we've, each of us, known for a long, long time.

The *San Diego Union-Tribune* came. A nice article in the Sunday paper, followed, of course, by letters to the editor suggesting that Paul and Lori's efforts among the forgotten should be forgotten as well, that any money paid to the teaching of these many murderers was better spent on swing sets for kids or food stamps for the hungry. The men knew, as should have those readers, that no money was spent, that givers made our Tuesday/Wednesday meetings in the prison happen, that our hope began in the golden rule, itself a hard kernel of thought, "unto" and "others" the only non-monosyllables in the whole damned deal.

And so the men took those letters to task. They wrote, and they wrote again, and they made those letters of indifference different.

They wrote them better, and then they showed us all how they had done it.

I crawled away that day.

ACKNOWLEDGEMENTS

This work would not exist without the cooperation and dedication of hundreds of men and women who shared our dream, including the administrative staff and officers at Richard J. Donovan Correctional Facility; the leadership and members of the Criminals and Gang Members Anonymous organization; the students from my corrections class at San Diego State University; writer and teacher—and dear, dear college classmate and friend—John E. Brown; and my dedicated and inspirational wife, Lori.

Prisons are understandably wary of outsiders and new programs. New wardens, even more so. But in RJD Warden Daniel Paramo, we found an enthusiastic champion. He not only welcomed us and our idea of a creative writing class during his first year as warden there, he allocated the staff and support resources to enable us to bring dozens of college students onto the maximum security yard of a prison unfamiliar with such intrusions both to "shadow" correctional staff and to work with the prisoners in our writing program over the course of several years. Public Information Officers Victor Sosa and Patrick Logan, and Community Resources Managers Frank Ruffino and Robert Brown were equally supportive, dedicating extensive parts of their days affording access to our classroom and our writers.

At the threshold of all of this—although never directly involved—was Richard M., founder of Criminals and Gang Members Anonymous (CGA), a prisoner self-help organization with chapters inside and outside of prisons across California. Because CGA is dedicated to changing prisoners' lives, Richard was supportive of my idea of getting prisoners to communicate more openly and honestly through the written word.

We first met during one of my weeklong, statewide PrisonTours that included Mule Creek State Prison, some 15 years before our writing class in RJD. We spoke briefly of such a class and experimented with the idea, long distance, as his CGA group in Mule Creek worked with my corrections class back in San Diego. That paved the way for the class in RJD. But Richard was never directly involved in the RJD class, due to his tragic and untimely death, even though he was transferred from Mule Creek to RJD.

After Richard's passing, his son, Peter, facilitated our access to the CGA chapter in RJD, where this volume, and our feature documentary chronicling this class, *Straight from the Pen,* were produced.

I am also thankful to my adventurous corrections students from SDSU who embraced the notion of sitting down, face to face, with a group of prisoners, mostly lifers, in an experiment that I hoped would open their minds to a world previously revealed to them only through their college texts and popular, mostly misleading, media depictions. The students were, no doubt, a welcome distraction to the prisoners' world, otherwise defined by the boredom and tedium that is prison. At the same time, however, most confessed apprehension at the idea of submitting their work to the judgment of college students when many of the prisoners, themselves, had never made it much past grade school.

Most importantly, of course, there would have been no students, no class, no book, and no movie had it not been for the courage of those men in blue who joined us in this experiment. A sad reality of incarceration is that the prison culture does not look kindly upon those who genuinely seek to improve themselves; and beyond that, openness, honesty, humility, and cooperation with "the man" (as we were regarded by many of those on the inside) are taken as signs of weakness or, worse, collusion, something which can jeopardize the physical safety of "collaborators." The men who participated in our classes were fully mindful of these facts—and were often reminded by guards and inmates, alike, lest they forget. But they joined us, nevertheless.

Aside from the physical and psychological harassment prisoners endured for their involvement, an even greater risk was the fear of failure. Incarcerated populations share one characteristic, perhaps, above all others—a cycle of failure. In school, in family, in inter-personal relationships, in employment, and a host of interactions that define their existence, failure has crippled their self-confidence and sense of worth, making them especially susceptible to the lure of gangs and crime and, at the same time, wary of self-exploration and psychological exposure.

Unfamiliar challenges threaten, even paralyze, such men. For most, wielding a gun or a knife amidst a gang of adversaries was easy, even empowering. Yet, wielding a pen in front of a class of college students, accomplished writers, and fellow convicts standing ready to "criticize" their efforts was downright terrifying.

Nevertheless, most rose to the challenge; with time, our classes became wildly successful and the men, ever so dedicated. Conspicuously, only one or two, and eventually none, of the prisoners actually took advantage of their routine evening dinner breaks which came in the middle of our four-hour classes. Said one, on behalf of the others, "We can always eat; but this class is once in a lifetime."

Many in our classes have now paroled or otherwise been released. We are constantly delighted to hear from them, as they return to a life among the rest of us. During our years at RJD, we received every bit as much from these men as they from us. Those of us "on the outside" will always be in their debt for what they taught us about life and humanity.

Ultimately, the soul behind much of the class was provided by my dear friend John E. Brown. John and I shared three formative years in Battenfeld Scholarship Hall on the campus of the University of Kansas. John grew up in a little farm town called Hoisington, about 200 miles east of my comparable home in Goodland, on the Kansas-Colorado border. At KU, John's mastery of both Milton and the English language impressed.

Thousands of miles and four decades intervened before a mutual Kansas buddy reunited us. I mentioned I had been thinking of doing a creative writing course in prison. John's no-words-wasted reply: "I'm in, sir." And the course for the next four years was set.

When John flew in from Wichita to San Diego for the opening and closing meetings of each class, he brought not only his unparalleled talent as a scribe, but more importantly, a compassion and love that inspired our writers to excel beyond the self-imposed limits of their talent. He truly loved these men—and they, him. And they blossomed.

Finally, my beloved Lori has at least equaled my energy and devotion in trying to bring something more to my students on both sides of the bars than can be found in traditional criminological texts. Just as she joined me for decades of weeklong excursions through scores of California prisons, she enthusiastically donned camera and microphone, pen and tablet, on this last academic adventure of ours before my retirement. She not only mentored and supported our writers for years—grading, correcting, and applauding their work—she photographed most the action for our already award-winning documentary about this class.

One lifer jokingly thanked Lori for the "pencil-whipping" she gave him on his first draft of one of the class's initial assignments. At the end of the course, the prisoners ceremoniously awarded Lori an honorary PhD for her loving devotion to the class and their lives. "Professor Lori," they call her now. Appropriately so.

For reminding us all that people are fundamentally good, and that people can change, we thank them all.

INTRODUCTION
L. Paul Sutton

Our classes at RJD focused on two major objectives—mastering the fundamentals of English composition and developing effective writing styles. To the first, we addressed the mechanics of writing—parts of speech, sentence structure, syntax, grammar, spelling, and punctuation.

Our underlying message to grown men who had little tolerance for grade-school grammar lessons was that a writer must respect his or her audience, their time, and their intellect. A badly written message will not only fail to persuade, it will fail to engage. And one's story will not matter if others will not read it. We urged our guys to attend to the mechanics of writing not merely for the sake of grammatical correctness, but because those skills are essential to getting people to respect them as writers, as people, and to care about what they have to say.

The second, even more important thrust of the class related to style. Effective writing must be more than literate; it must captivate. People do not pick up a book to grade it for spelling and punctuation. Audiences read to be moved, involved, inspired, entertained. They read to feel something, to feel alive, to feel human. Effective writing whisks the reader—exploiting his senses of sight, sound, smell, taste, and touch—into the writer's world, to watch a movie play out in words.

We suggested four rules for good writing:
1. Use concrete, specific nouns. (Detail, not vagaries.)
2. Use strong, active verbs. (Show action; avoid "to be" forms.)
3. Show, don't tell. (Help the reader to "experience" the action.)
4. Simplest is best. (Good writing is straight forward.)
   a. Omit needless words. (Avoid fillers and redundancy.)
   b. Avoid fancy words. (Bigger is not always better.)

Additionally, we practiced strategies like varying sentence length; using compound versus simple sentences, and using sentence structure to create or subordinate emphasis.

My years of teaching upper-division college students have taught me (1) that most people, including many faculty, are poor writers and (2) that this is due, in large part, to the naïve writer's mistaken notion that "fancy" and "wordy" impute insight or intellect. They think, for example, that the word "utilize" somehow communicates more than the word "use." I was reminded of my KU English 101 professor's admonition: "Never utilize 'utilize!' 'Use' is a perfectly fine verb. So *use* it!" And, he added, "that damned thesaurus is a bane to good writing. So, *lose* it!"

John Brown's inevitable refrain, upon hearing a suspiciously thesaurus-doctored construction: "Would you say that on the yard? Have your ever heard anyone talk like that on the yard?" Our rule was *keep it simple*. You don't have to dazzle to impress; indeed, simplicity can be elegant.

One final rule: your first draft is just that—a draft. Good writing is the product of writing and re-writing. After several iterations at the table, the guys would read their essays to the entire class, get feedback, and then re-write some more.

Most significantly, this class helped these men with more than just their writing. I believe it taught them that, by applying themselves, they could improve not only their essays, but their lives. And, further, it taught them that they could do it for themselves, by themselves: they did not have to rely on anyone but themselves. Writing was challenging, to be sure; but the rewards were powerful and immediate—rarities in prison. They found success—some, for the first time in years.

Ultimately, our aim was to help them find a voice with which to tell their stories, to give life to their experiences so that others could better understand who they were.

So, what to write about? No doubt, these men had stories to tell—incredible, tragic, horrific, sad, even funny. Indeed, the majority had spent most of their lives doing crime and paying for it. They came from varied backgrounds of wealth, poverty, abuse, neglect, solitude, failure, despair, gangs, violence, even many stripes of love. Our aim was to get them to open up and write about familiar, albeit painful, topics about which they had plenty to say—if only they could find the courage to open up. We never asked them to write specifically about their crimes, unless they were pertinent to the assigned topic.

We generally assigned one-word topics intended to get them to look into themselves, to better understand themselves, their values, their strengths, weaknesses, and shortcomings. Specifically, we asked them to write about things like insecurity, love, hate, deceit, remorse, death, loneliness, friendship, family, loyalty, respect, honesty, hopes, and dreams. We also assigned four short subjects—"my first day," "my 10-year old self," and, in honor of two holidays, "Halloween" and "Christmas." Each topic produced a broad and unpredictable array of essays, as the imaginations of these men blossomed.

Ultimately, their essays, regardless of topic, revealed experiences, themes, threads, and "life courses," as criminologists call them, that these men tended to share. Accordingly, we present the following essays as a gripping portrayal of the lives, thinking, and evolution, of not only these men, but of their counterparts locked up in prisons across the land.

PART 1. GROWING UP

There is no greater agony than bearing an untold story inside you.

- Maya Angelou

OPENING DOORS
Jose C.

I wake up to the sound of a dumpster truck backing up after collecting some trash. I go check on my 3 siblings still sleeping, all under 5 years old.

I sneak out, lock the doors, and go to the nearest store to steal our morning breakfast—maybe a box of Ninja Turtle candies. Moms is at Fallbrook slinging dope to pay the rent. She's been gone three days now.

Uncle Raymond calls the police on Moms. She gots his car in exchange for meth and a verbal contract, but he says she stole it. He also mentions she left her children all alone at our apartment.

Back at the pad, I'm playing Zelda with my siblings. I am searching through villages for an item to jump higher, allowing me to go to the next level. My little brother has the other controller, but it's unplugged. He thinks he is a game genius. "Go Henry! You're doing great."

The phone calls me away. I pause Zelda and run to it, leaving Henry confused, 'cause the elf is not moving to his command.

"Hello?"

"Mijo, don't open the door to no one. Remember what I taught you."

"Yes, Mom."

I hang up and lock the door. I run back to watching my brother, but now he's banging his controller on the floor. I press the start button and we are back to conquering the world.

"Knock, knock," The baby wakes up. I run to the door, excited to see my mom.

"Joey!" I stop inches from the door. "It's the police, Joey!"

Adrenaline rushing, I practice and train for 20 minutes of tuff negotiations. I hear the voice that brings me back to my 10-year-old self.

"Mijo, it's Mommy." I open the door to my first day in the foster care system.

FIELDER'S CHOICE
George B.

The sound of the shot made me take my eye off the fly ball headed my way. A scream of pain came from nearby. The ball threaded through the grass as I ran with the rest of my team toward the sounds of chaos. Boys shot! Smoking tires screamed as cars on the roadway slid to a halt. Drivers blasted their horns protesting the delay on journeys home.

An agonizing cry of pain from a dark-skinned man. As he tried to stand, blood flowed dark against the ebony fingers of his empty hand. His other arm hung limply at his side, holding a chromed .32 revolver pointed at the ground. The two men circled their crumpled vehicles, stalking each other. One held the gun, the other—two white-handled switchblades, dripping crimson. The second man, white shirt emblazed with two bright red splotches, his torso holed by bullets.

Sirens of police cars in the distance, we slowed our rush from the ball field, drawn to this scene from the Inferno. The men rushed each other. As they grappled, one more shot tore through the cacophony of sounds surrounding the combatants. The assailant in white stabbed again and again, each blow misting the air with scarlet. The gunman slumped to his knees. Life coarsened though his fingers, a frothy bright-red foam.

Cops! Guns pointed everywhere, even at me. "Freeze!" they ordered. "Get on the ground!" "Roll over!" yelled another, as he cuffed the dying man, blood roiling from the repeated knife wounds. Hands held high, the other driver protested, "He shot me! He shot me!"

Dropping the blade, he fell to his knees, guns pointed at his head. He, too, was cuffed. Ambulance attendants put the wounded man on a gurney. The gunman was clearly dead, face in the gutter. I heard two blue cops talking. The first said, "The dead guy ran outta' bullets." His cohort responded, "Yeah, the other guy didn't run outta' knife."

My dad later that day asked me what I thought about witnessing my first death, if I'd learned anything. "Yes", I told him, "If you're gonna shoot somebody, use a bigger gun."

FAMILY WAGON
Oscar G.

Sitting on your lap, I remember turning the steering wheel with your guiding hand. We're going fast, but not as fast as the time you were drunk and kidnapped my little sister, and my mom chased you in another car. We fly down the highway, past tumbleweeds and vultures as Guns N' Roses crashes inside our van, on our way to Sin City—so my father could gamble and we could call it a family vacation.

Our first stop is the nearest casino. So my dad could have some fun, we are left to be babysat by Homer and Marge Simpson in some dingy hotel room, which wasn't that different from my babysitter at home, "Barney." Later, we stroll down the open-roofed Venetian hallways, where I've never seen a sky so clear and blue. Then, it's the pirate show, where they fight tooth and nail—kinda like my parents.

Even through all the bad, I looked up to you. I believe everything you tried to do for us was with sincere affection towards the whole family.

GANGSTER: DAY ONE
Patrick A.

A hazy L.A. sun sets on my thirteenth year, painting the thick concrete of Juvenile Hall a dreary gray. Far from my first night away from home, it's my first in jail. The first in detention blue, one-size-fits-all stretch pants. The first with hostile lips standing before me in a baggy white-T and slick hair reeking of too much Tres Flores pomade, kissing through a clutch of crooked teeth clenched and demanding, "Donde eres, ése?"

"Where am I from…" echoes in my head and throughout unit J, where the bodies of throw-away kids graffiti the baby bench lining the wall. My father, my uncles, and even my cousins would rush to answer in a flare of defiant pride, but not me. I'm not from a gang.

In the silence between us, the hiss grows red-eyed and vicious, pressing an answer. Fear and anxiety creep up my back, "Rosemead," takes a running start across my tongue and bellyflops on the dirty linoleum at my feet.

A sick twitch of amusement plays at the corner of the wall of teeth and I notice one's missing. "No, pendejo! What varrio?"

From across the room a voice rang out, "He's not from the hood, but he's my little homeboy." Two fists and a teardrop tattoo, still red from the sharpened paper clip cuts through the graffiti to say, "You mess with him, you mess with me!"

WHATCHAM
Eric O.

School stretches on through the day as I stare at a clock that lives on dead batteries. How long is this going to last? Finally! The bell screams, waking up a sleeping giant. I dash to my getaway bike, dodging any chance at extra work or detention. I narrowly escape the closing gates of school, and expertly ride off into the abyss.

First, I gather my boys—the Mighty Four. Youth on our side, the world is ours. Tall eucalyptus trees are no match; rooftops are overrun by our dusty footprints; abandoned buildings are hours of fun, stretching longer than train smoke, swinging on ropes above water-filled storm drains.

The city, my playground. I lived up the steepest dead-end, the "ghetto Mount Everest," which led to lopsided baseball and football games; paper–rocks–scissors to chase the ball a mile down the street. No care in the world, we were good at being kids. School clothes became street clothes with one catch and dive into the mud. I was the king of my domain, and "fun" was the name of our gang. Neighborhood feuds were as foreign to me as the lifestyles of the rich and famous. Girls might as well have been from another planet. Free as a kid was as free as can be.

NO SWEAT
Jose C.

Behind the Circle "K," there's a small field with high bushes. Beyond the thick wall of sticks, there's an area with a creek filled with crawdads. My brother and I claimed it as our own. We would go there often to get away from reality. It felt as if walking through the branches would magically transport us to a fantasy world; but instead of a talking lion, it would be an occasional field worker sleeping next to a 24 pack. Lucky for us, we mastered the art of playing He-Man, Thunder Cats, and G.I Joe in silence from growing up in a house of alcoholics.

Having a big brother was awesome. Everyone knew him as Franky, but it could have been Baby because that's what moms would call him. Even some of his girlfriends called him that. When we got in trouble, he always cried; so even I called him Baby. We explored the world together. We climbed the highest mountains east of Rainbow, searching the caves of the Middle Earth—better know by the villagers as the Fallbrook sewage system.

One time he woke me up in the middle of the night. "Joey, it's time to take one for your big brother."

He was dressed up with his clothes backwards like Kris Kross, so I did what little brothers do and copied him. We moved expertly like Navy Seals through the living room full of King Cobra land mines to the balcony, where we jumped off—cause that was more exciting.

We walked all the way to Live Oak Park to meet up with his girlfriend and her little sister. "Joey when we get there, keep her little sister busy... alright?" We passed the bathrooms and next to the swings stood the most beautiful girl I'd ever seen. I walked up to her, "Hi, I'm Joey." My brother walked away with his girlfriend, looked back at me and said, "You owe me one bro." The night was cold; I was hungry and my feet hurt, but I got my first kiss. A night I'll never forget.

"Mr. Cuen!" I snap out of my daydream, "Yeah," "Do you understand the plea bargain you signed?" I look across the courtroom at Franky crying next to his lawyer. What a baby, every time we get in trouble. "Yes. I get 18 years and my brother goes home." My lawyer asks me, "Mr. Cuen why are you doing this for him." I look at him then look at Franky, "Why wouldn't I? He's my big brother."

A NEW FAMILY
Tam N.

Punches and kicks rained down on my head and body as I lay curled in a protective ball. Earlier, I had tried fighting back, but two bear-like Samoans body-slammed all sense of resistance out of me. Every blow shook my mind like an earthquake. My body began to go numb.

Though my body wouldn't respond to my commands, my mind and senses were clear and sharp as ever. I could hear the labored breathing by my attackers and the shouts of joy from bystanders. I saw the creased dark-blue Dickies and scuffed Chuck Taylors of the attacker closest to me as he kicked me. Peeking through my fingers I noticed gang tagging on a dirty wall. The sharp, rank smell of crack mingled with urine on the cold gray cement floor I lay on.

Suddenly, the blows stopped. I was raised to my feet and embraced by a crowd of people like they would a long-lost brother. I wiped blood from my nose and mouth. I felt a welt under my left eye. Then a short, stocky, black-skinned Cambodian handed me a black baseball cap with Old English stitching on the front that read "Long Beach CBC". He told me "We're your brothers now".

At that time I couldn't help but think of my father. What if I hadn't broken his rules and gotten kicked out of his home? For a moment I felt self-pity for being a homeless 14-year-old that no one cared for. But, as I looked around me at all the youths with gang tattoos, sharing alcohol and laughing, I realized I wasn't alone anymore. I had a new family.

A STRUGGLE FROM THE START
Robert G.

January 28, 1975—a bittersweet day for my family. My mother started going into labor; she was rushed to the hospital to give birth to a baby boy. Everything became serious once she had arrived and started receiving medical attention at Charter Community Hospital in Lakewood, California.

Prior to this day, she had not been receiving prenatal care due to a disagreement between my father and her. But this day, as she prepared to give birth, she began struggling with her own life. Medical staff started running tests to explain complications my mother was having. Tests revealed that the baby's heart was not beating correctly: there was a hole in the heart, and the baby had a murmur.

Our family were told about these complications, that there was a chance that my mother may not survive, but that the baby might be saved. With God's grace, my mother lived and the baby was born. But it needed immediate medical attention due to the heart defect and jaundiced condition.

My mother and father were alcohol and drug abusers; tests revealed that my mother was under the influence when she arrived at the hospital.

An innocent baby boy, a struggle for life from the start: my first day, and high on heroin.

TEETH
Cesar L.

Row upon row of pearly whites; our family photo's were a sight to see. But then, there stood me, serious as can be. Smile for the birdie; everyone say "cheese!". No sir, not for me. Adolescent years were a serious affair. My smile, for the most part, was non-existent. Caught in a culture that thrived on looks, I felt I'd fall short, rewarding it with ammunition.

Finally came my mustache-to-be. Oh how I thanked God for that hair above my lip, combing and cultivating it, just so it would hide the teeth I didn't want anyone to see.

Until one day my heart skipped a beat. She was beautiful with a smile so sweet. Standing amongst a group of guys, I looked to my left, then to my right. All around, Cheshire grins were out for full effect. I was crestfallen. How could I compete? With nothing more to offer, I was just me.

One by one, they began to fall. That's when I noticed she came toward me. She asked my name; I didn't reply. She said, "Why so serious? Or are you just shy?"

Wouldn't you like to know the end of it all? By the end of the night, I was 10ft tall. And there we stood for all the world to see. Smiling like a fool, my gapped teeth and me.

LONELY HOOPS
Jojo D.

Daybreak. Stressed out, I drove to the park to clear my thoughts. Walking to a bench I noticed a small Asian boy, alone, quietly shooting hoops, missing every shot.

I approach him. "Are you ok?" No reply, just a sad nod. To cheer him up, I ask, "Can I shoot hoops with you?" Still, no reply; but lonely, abandoned eyes hand me the ball.

Shockwaves of memories flash through my body as I touch the leather ball, reeling me back to my early childhood. I am blinded by bright light and tortured by screams of "Dog eater!" "Stupid Chinaman." And "Go back to China!" They attacked maliciously, their words stabbing harder than punches or kicks.

Balled up with hands wrapped around knees and head tucked to chest, I cry, "Dad, where are you? I need you! I'm scared." My heart erupts lava-like, spilling hot ache, hardened by rejection and chilled from abuse.

Memories fade to chirps and sunshine, tears running down my face. In the middle of the court, soft, pale hands wipe my salty tears away. "It's ok. I know your pain" whispered the 10-year-old boy. Recognizing his soft brown Asian eyes and button nose, I smile. He hugs me, then disappears.

Thank you for healing my ruptured heart.

EL SALVADOR
Edwin C.

Hot lead rains from every roof top. The peaceful avenue cracks, violently slicing the air between my 5 years and Mother's outstretched hand as El Salvador erupts.

Mother screams into shell-shocked silence, gathering my brothers and sister to the temporary shelter of a concrete wall. Making herself small, she desperately pounds a nearby door. Bodies grunt lifelessly to the pavement with each bang of her fist.

"Por favor" bleeds from my mama's knuckles, beseeching the stranger on the safe side of a thick, rust-colored door. "Tengo mis hijos." An old woman's tired eyes slowly cracked the door, just enough to lend us her tidy wooden floor for the night. Echoes of war whip across the stars, stealing innocent lives.

In the morning, the war woke us, pulling back our blanket of security and we ran. We all ran, every one of us, in every direction. Alone, I ran into an intersection of empty buses and open car doors with motors running. I couldn't understand the lack of movement or why cars were parked in the middle of the street.

Turning, I tripped over a child's bloody body, landing face to face with her frozen eyes, lightly dusted and dull. Afraid to move, afraid they might blink, I laid in the eerie calm of diesel motors dying.

A few minutes seemed an eternity before a soldier pulled me to my feet and made them walk through the broken dreams and bloated bodies. He took me to a church where I found my family, and he left.

Three days later, he joined those bloated bodies on the street. I never knew his name. But to me, he was my guardian angel from a living hell.

WRESTLE MANIA
Patrick A.

C ome, dear reader, peer through the bedroom window and see a 10-year-old boy balled up on a royal blue carpet, all the fight stripped of him before breakfast. Follow me for yet a closer look; let us climb through the window he'll someday use to escape into the night before awakening in prison. Hush...lest we disturb. Stand fast beside me and watch. Not fifteen minutes ago, he sat in the living room, rather pleased he'd scored the best seat in the house to watch cartoons.

"Go to your room, Chief." His words drifted from the couch toward the tweed-green rocking chair landing square in my pajama'd lap. So nonchalant, they floated across the dimly-lit room, I thought them not for me. How could they be? How could I be in trouble before "Good Morning"?

"Chief, I said go to your room," rumbled from beside my mother, this time not so nice.

"Why?" I plead, the words dripping. "But it's Saturday." Every Saturday morning, my family gathered in the front room before the only television to watch Bugs Bunny make way for Hulk Hogan's 24-inch pythons, figure-four leg locks, and neck-crunching pile drivers.

"I didn't do anything wrong," ventured from my blanket, still warm of sleep. "Go!" sliced the room in half. Less than a whisper, two tons of "No" lumbered upon the edge of my lip ... and fell.

Sorry the second I spoke, but too late to call back, the letters rang through the house. In the booming echo, he darted past my little sister, her frightened eyes clutching an over-sized bowl of Frosted Flakes, snatched my foot, and dragged me, rug burned, to my bedroom. Spilling me in the middle of the floor, he turned and closed the door behind us.

Body slammed against walls, choking beneath his forearm, and pile-driven to the ground, I prayed my mother would dropkick the wall, tag in, and save me. She didn't.

Finding my feet, I peered at him defiantly, refusing to tap out.

THE CYCLE
Brian L.

I was a typical teenager, thinking I had it all figured out. Yet, I suffered from a desire so powerful—to be accepted and feel loved—that I compromised myself to satisfy it.

It began with changing myself, just a little here and there. These changes were never so great that I felt like a liar or a fraud, but a compromise of character, none-the-less; and each time I gave up ground, before I realized it, the cycle of madness would begin. It was so innocent. I just wanted acceptance and love, but that's not what I ended up with; the cycle wouldn't allow it.

I felt like I was inferior, and it made me anxious. The fear of rejection and judgment followed closely, revealing my every flaw. Next would come the twists and turns of compromise. Always changing to fit in, doing whatever it took to please others. Drinking? Sure! Drugs? Let's do it! Robbery? Violence? I was down for it all, just as long as I was accepted. But inside, I moved farther and farther from who I really wanted to be.

So I changed more to be more like them, to fit in better. They would accept me if I was better at being them than they were. But with each compromise came more fear, doubt, shame, and anxiety. So I would change more to escape those feelings until I reached the breaking point.

These emotions infected all of my relationships. Fear, the emotional cancer—fear of judgment, fear of rejection, fear of failure, even fear of success. I tortured myself over imagined disrespect. I analyzed each word spoken to me for hidden meanings. I sought out the insults in compliments and looked for the judgments that existed only in my fear-fevered thoughts.

Nothing I feared was truthful or factual, but I reacted as if it were. I rejected others before they could reject me. I convinced myself I'm better off alone and, with my fears fulfilled, I felt justified in my doubt-torn mind, convincing myself I would have ended up the same way—alone.

It's taken tremendous work to find a solution--an exit strategy, so to speak, from the cycle of madness. I learned that I had issues so big that my issues had their own issues. I learned that it's what I do in spite of the chaos. I have found that forgiveness is the only true path. So my answer is to forgive myself as best as I can and to offer to others what I so desperately wanted—Love and Acceptance.

NOT SMART ENOUGH
Joe A.

As my fourth grade teacher passed out our report cards, she made brief comments like, "Good job" or "I'll miss you!" We all clapped and waited for the next name. Mine was last. I don't know why. She said they were in alphabetical order.

Mrs. Alvarez looked at me and said, "Jose, you pass, but not because you deserve it. I just don't want you in my class anymore. You're not smart enough! I'll let Mr. Mendevil deal with you."

I sat and stared at her, unsure what to do. My ears were ringing from the laughter around me, as some of the kids called me dumb. I sat there, head down, staring at my hands. I clenched my fists, my fingernails digging into my palms. I feel the tears burning in my eyes. I knew I had to fight them back: crying would only make it worse.

This was the end of my second year in Mrs. Alvarez's class. I had to repeat it because my English wasn't good enough. I had tried so hard! Maybe she's right: I will never be smart.

I rose and made my way through the aisle, the laughter and words still pounding around me. Pretending not to care, I laughed along with my tormentors.

That night, as I lay in bed, the words pounded in my head. "You're just not smart enough! You're just not smart enough!" I was angry, not at my teacher or even at the other kids, but at myself. Why was I so dumb? Why did I always fail? What was wrong with me?

Angry and confused, I wanted never to feel that way again. I had learned a valuable lesson from Ms. Alvarez: I was just not smart enough. So I decided not to try and not to care. Indifference became my armor, shielding me from the pain of what would be a life of failures.

FEEL MY PAIN, HEAR MY CRIES
David B.

I was molested when I was 10 or 11. Carl had made me feel safe at first. He was very nice, almost like a big brother. He would lie next to me on the floor, and for months that's all he would do, so I felt comfortable, like we were having a sleepover. The sleepovers ended after Carl molested me. I knew what he did to me was not right and definitely not normal, and I was ashamed for even allowing it to happen. Carl told me not to tell anyone. I was scared, so didn't tell a soul.

I was never really the same after that. I was very uncomfortable around people, especially men. I didn't trust anyone; I thought everyone had an ulterior motive or would harm me in some way, especially sexually.

About a year after I was molested, I was attending church with a friend of mine who was a couple of years older. Keyon was well versed in the Bible, and I really admired him. He was like a big brother. One Sunday, I went over to Keyon's house. While I was waiting for him to get ready for church, he came out of the bedroom and asked me if he could perform oral sex on me. I ran out of that house and wanted nothing more to do with God.

I began to question everything. Here I was, all of twelve years old, and I had been molested by a "big brother" figure, and now another "big brother" figure is wanting to give me oral sex. Is something wrong with me? Am I inviting these situations in my life? I was confused and unsure of who or what I was.

I began drinking heavily, sniffing paint, and smoking marijuana daily. I even hung with my Mexican friend and his street gang for a few months. I was out of control. I was doing all I could to forget Carl and Keyon and how they hurt me.

While hanging with this gang, I was arrested for a stolen car. The cops asked me for my dad's name. It turned out they actually knew him—not in a good way. For the first and only time in my entire life, I saw a picture of my dad—hanging in the Los Angeles Newton Police Station. They told me he lived on 27th and Central. That hurt because I had lived on 42nd and Central all my life, and I'd never seen my dad. All I could think was that he didn't love me, and I felt worthless.

I started asking questions about my biological mother. I found out she was a drug addict and a prostitute and in and out of prison. I would soon see my mother barefoot in the street. All I could think was that she didn't love me, either.

I felt a void in my life. I tried to fill it by stealing, vandalizing, and trying to have as many girlfriends as possible.

In 1999, my mother and I both paroled from prison, and she moved in with my grandmother and me. One day, my mother's boyfriend stepped out of her room naked to grab the phone off the ironing board. I got upset, kicked my mom's bedroom door in and challenged the dude to a fight. My girlfriend hugged me tight and said, "Let it go, forgive her." Truth be told, I wasn't mad at my mother's boyfriend. I was mad at my mother for having the audacity to have a boyfriend. I felt like she shouldn't have time for anyone but me.

I was both unsure of myself and felt sorry for myself. I blamed everyone from my molesters to my mom and dad for the way my life turned out. I even blamed my mother for my womanizing ways. Three weeks before my grandmother passed, her last words to me were, "Forgive your mother."

And I did. I have come to understand that I must be in control of how I feel, and I have the capacity to make good and moral decisions. No one else is to blame for the mistakes I made. I now accept responsibility for all my choices.

I am even grateful for all my experiences, because I feel like everything happens for a reason. Without struggle, there is no progress. My hope is that by sharing my experiences, I can bring strength, insight, and hope to someone else.

To whomever may read this, may God bless you. Be encouraged knowing that weeping may fill the night, but joy comes in the morning. (Psalm 30:5)

SHARE THE DREAM
Mark P.

Growing up, I had little time for hopes or dreams. My life called for me to be in the here and now—surviving drug-abusing parents and total dysfunction in my home. Dreams were thngs that came during sleep, and hope seemed pointless.

As a small, scared child, I hoped mostly that I would one day have a normal family, with loving parents. I wished for all my brothers and sisters to live under one roof. I often imagined myself as someone else's child, inventing my role in my new family. I would always be the favorite.

I still daydream about what life would be like had personal tragedy not visited. What if my grandma hadn't died? What if my brother hadn't been killed? I long to know the answers.

Now, my hopes and dreams are different. I hope for a better life, where it's alright to have dreams. My dream is to live in peace and to instill in my children the importance of compassion, forgiveness, and honest work. I encourage them to share the spiritualism I have tried to teach. I dream of happiness, laughter, joy, and serenity.

THE APPLE OF MY EYE
Oscar M.

I loved kindergarten. School was a sunny blast, a wonderland. My teacher was pretty and the tricycle that I got to ride was neat. Then, the unforeseen gripped me, as a dark, gloomy pattern emerged. I was overwhelmed by failure. I was different: I was mentally slow, seemingly unable to learn. The little self-worth and confidence that I had known was drowned in a pool of my own tears.

I fell into the dilapidated cracks of an overworked school system. I became a negative statistic. A once-happy little boy, I now wondered: was I bred solely for failure, an animal that would buckle under the pressure of life? The yoke of illiteracy forced me to withdraw.

My third grade teacher, Sherry, was a beautiful person. I treasure her memory, having loved her gentle and loving approach. Clearly and uniquely, she cared.

I remember with bittersweet clarity the day that I was promoted out of her class, and forced into the fourth grade. Daily, I would eagerly reappear in her class, waiting, wanting, longing to be readmitted. She was more than patient; she was loving. To her embarrassment, I made her my school mom, as I clung desperately to fill my own emptiness.

Unready to break ties or move on, I was often dragged off as a trespasser by male teachers, and even once, by the janitor. But I was undeterred. Emotionally, I was helpless, longing for warmth and acceptance.

Finally, she was forced to take action, knowing that I would otherwise never leave her doorstep nor her side. She had patiently fed my hungry soul with hope. While her words were stern, they quivered with compassion. But all I felt was the slap of rejection. I had to go.

Grade after grade, I found nothing but defeat and the excruciating pain of failure. I felt weak and preyed upon. I was hunted down with questions I could not answer. The laughter of my classmates became my judgment. The incessant bombardment forced me to take cover, as I found temporary shelter at the back of the class.

Darkness hovered. Who was I meant to be? How was I to survive? My desperation ripened into defiance. I crawled out from behind my desk and into a violent future. I became a monster. The dummy blossomed with hate. And the torturous laughter stopped.

Today, after a lifetime in the dark, I can see the peaking sun, as I feel God's warmth. An eagle I must be, for I now soar high upon the backs of dreams, on an uplifting current of hope. I pray for God's healing touch upon everyone like the boy I was.

NO SHAME IN THAT
Patrick A.

My puffy brown and tan nylon jacket was a slightly stained hand-me-down from a cousin who had long outgrown it. It was my favorite jacket throughout the 3rd grade, because I could unzip its sleeves to form a vest. The material's smooth sheen gave way to a geometric zigzag pattern that reminded me of what someone might wear to a ski lodge. It could be worn in any weather; and importantly, it was bulky and covered my waist. When I wore my vest, no one could tell I was a little fat kid.

Hand-me-downs from thrift stores and yard sales were common for my family. There is no shame in that...or so I was told. Sometimes I'd even get lucky with a Harley-Davidson t-shirt or some sports paraphernalia, even a concert shirt. Instant vintage, right?

I wore a pea-green Philadelphia Eagles T-shirt, a Pittsburgh Steelers beanie, and carried a slightly banged-up Dukes of Hazzard lunch pail with a mismatched Scooby Doo thermos that I'd scored for a quarter. No, there's no shame in that.

I was a big kid, a fat boy, or, as the sales lady kindly called me, "husky." When the new school year would roll around, and everyone else was out shopping for the latest fashion, I was collecting used clothes or ducking into the husky boys' department.

Pants were always too long because my waist was too round. My pants had to be hemmed up a few inches to allow for growth. I never got used to this, especially with my Levi's, because every month or so, the hem had to be let out a little and re-sewn. The tell-tale sign of a faded line marking the previous hem would rest just above my bargain brand, Buy-One-Get-One-Free, Payless Shoes.

I would complain, "But Mom, the other kids are going to make fun of me!" Mom would soothingly say, "They are perfectly good pants, and there is no shame in that."

Defeated, I would convince myself that everything was as it should be. I'd show up for the first day of school with my stained brown jacket/vest, thrift store tee, twice let-out Levi's and Dukes of Hazzard lunch box.

What was wrong with me? Others fit in so well while I had to struggle to make the grade. They had the best toys, listened to the right music, wore the current fashions, said the right things, and knew the right people. It all seemed so easy for them. They were cool: I wasn't.

Why was I so different? And…why didn't anyone ever tell me that I was just "normal?" 'Cause there's no shame in that, either.

THE YELLOW SUIT
Johnny S.

A boy scout at 13. An outstanding deacon in the church. I was even baptized for the dead in a Mormon temple in the big city of Salt Lake, Utah. Women from the church offered words of praise to my grandmother. "He is such a good boy, I wish my son was more like him." I would beam with joy, but never in the open. Hearing those comments would almost make me feel bad, selling people pigeons without clipping their wings. Once released, they would fly back home.

I was often invited to family outings—fishing and camping trips with families not my own. Yet I felt like a trusted family member.

Sunday morning. I can hear my grandmother going from room to room yelling, loudly banging on walls and doors with her broom. That broom was her little sidekick and her weapon of choice. My grandmother was very strong and independent. She loved her kids and her church. Sunday was a special day set aside for God. God helps those who help themselves. On this day, she would not hesitate waking you with a few hard taps from her faithful friend, like a magic wand.

Church day was my favorite day of the week. Finding something to wear wasn't difficult: I owned only one suit. My grandmother bought it from the Goodwill on First street—a bright, canary yellow suit with dark brown polka dots, a few sizes too big for me. I hated that suit.

Passing out communion was a part of my responsibility as a deacon. And people would always hand me envelopes to deliver to the Bishop's office—ten percent of their weekly earnings. During the second half of church, I'd take a short walk to the 7-11 for a big bag of ruffles and a cold 7-Up. One day, I was handed more envelopes than I've ever been given at one time. Being in such a hurry to get to their seats, they had forgotten to drop off their envelopes. But never too far away in his yellow suit was their faithful servant. God helps those who help themselves.

Happy with myself on how great the day turned out, I was celebrating my good fortune in the parking lot when I was summoned to the Bishop's office. My bright and sunny day suddenly turned gray.

My smile disappeared as I stood before the Bishop, trying to marshal a look of innocence. I denied any knowledge of the missing envelopes. I was freed to return home with a pocket full of money, only to face my grandmother's wrath and her notorious broom.

Shocked... I was arrested for armed robbery. Found in my possession were an assortment of custom wedding rings and gold chains—a few items I had picked up during those family outings.

I was told that stealing money from the church is stealing from God. I confessed all my sins against God and the church. But the lesson was clear: God helps those who help themselves.

FINDING ME
Tyrone H.

I sat in the back of my fourth-grade class wishing I were invisible. I could smell my nervousness seeping through my pores. My mouth was filled with saliva, yet my throat was bone-dry: I couldn't swallow. My heart was pounding so fast I snuck a look at the person next to me, certain she could hear it. My palms were sweaty and I clenched my pencil so tightly I thought it would break.

The teacher was quizzing us, randomly, on math. "12-times-12," she rang out. I sank further into my seat. I knew the answer, but was afraid to raise my hand. I thought, "What if, somehow, I'm wrong?" The smell of pencil lead, chalk, Crayolas, books, and the body odor of two dozen fourth graders made me nauseous.

Anxiety stricken, I couldn't breathe. My teeth, hands, and feet were clenched; my empty stomach hurt. I could hear the constant words of my parents: "You'll never amount to nothing." "You're just like your father." "Nobody gives a shit about you." "You're different." "Keep your mouth shut!"

I raised my hand. "Yes, Tyrone?" the teacher asked, thinking I wanted to answer the question. "May I be excused?"

Granted permission, I ran out the front door of the school. I kept running, sweat pouring down my body, afraid to look back. I got home, ran to my room, grabbed my pillow, and curled up in the middle of my bed, shaking and crying, wondering why nobody cared for me. Why was I even born? At that moment I couldn't believe my parents loved me; seeing the affection other parents showed their kids, I wanted to be someone else. Rocking on my bed and crying, I felt like I was the only kid going through this and began to believe the things they'd said were true.

Shame filled my life, being the child of drug-addicted parents on welfare. I can still taste the awful sweetness of the blue chip stamps, those wrinkled books serving as our Christmas currency! Lay away, block cheese, and canned peanut butter. Kids teased, "You poor because your mama and daddy on the needle!" Humiliated by people I thought were my friends! They made me angry—angry because I was afraid, afraid because what they were saying was true, and powerless because I couldn't do anything to change it.

These feelings of abandonment, rejection, and fear made it practically impossible for me to forge healthy relationships. I didn't trust anyone because everyone I trusted had betrayed me. I believed all the painful things my addicted parents would say. No one had any expectations of me, so I had none for myself. My transition to a life of crime seemed logical.

I believed gang violence and criminal acts would show everyone I was worthy of attention. I used violence to cover my fear of being discovered to be the lonely, needful person I really was. I needed so desperately to feel the love of someone...of my parents.

All the things I wanted—to be loved, needed, cared for, accepted—I didn't know how to obtain. And that compounded my anger, knowing what I wanted and not being able to get it.

After a lifetime of self-loathing and self-pity, it has been through the help of others that I've learned to face myself, to quiet my inner destructive voices, and to change my thinking.

Having people in my life who genuinely encourage and help me to do—and be—better keeps me on the road to recovery. With their guidance, I have learned to believe in myself and to accept who I am.

BASEBALL
Victor G.

Half my life, I've been in prison. My twenty-eight year-old body sits in a circle with men who have all paid their tithe at the alter of violence. I learn that change is possible, and my hope is to break the cycle.

The photos hung high along the gym wall, the all-important in one sport or another. Coach was focused on a black and white of a tall, slinky man. "That's Ted Williams, the greatest hitter to ever step onto a diamond. He went to school here, walked the same streets you do. You guys could be up there with Ted if you want. But it's going to take a lot of work and dedication." Coach would always say things like that.

1992: The memory is forever be tattooed on my mind. Playing a sport went from something I dreamed about to something I aimed to do. Thinking back, I imagine that coach must have known the tug of war that would take place in our lives, since the barrio never passes on a generation. But for that moment, I believed him: I would eat and breathe baseball. And one day, I would be up there with Ted.

1995: the photos were different. They adorned a broken-down apartment complex that I passed to and from school. The figures were not like Ted and the others. Their skin was blue and green, their heads bald, their clothes nicely pressed. Their shoes looked like dust went around them. They, too, went to our school and walked our streets.

"What's up, little homie?" The acknowledgement made me feel cool and fearful at the same time. I nodded back, and with that nod, my grip on the rope slipped, my dream of one day being up there with Ted, buried in the mud. I became just another body holding up a broken-down apartment. I worked hard, dedicating myself to becoming a ghetto super star.

GANGSTER QUEEN
Patrick A.

Beyond her scarred knuckles and skank I-hope-you-do attitude, beyond her jawbreaker exterior and rattlesnake talk, there's a tenderoni before she became 'round the way.

Dolly-clothes innocent and latch-key neglect grew up fast in a concrete playground of graffiti streets, where liking one of her brother's gangster friends meant laying beneath him on a dusty beige couch in her girlfriend's garage. It meant trusting his practiced whisper of, "Don't worry, I got you," while his hand slowly slid down her shivering belly and snaked beyond white cotton panties.

Young and pregnant, she floats from funeral to funeral where her kindergarten friends fill pine boxes, and baby's daddies sport prison blue. A single mother, her men earn life sentences in a haze of meth smoke, landing her broken fingers, busted lips, and a smashed heart. Pig-tail sweetness and sing-song smiles fade till she's twisted and crunched up, crammed into Misery's Hall of Fame.

Wrapped in ghetto fabulous, she sits upon a throne of polished low-riders and Boulevard Knights wearing a crown of broken hearts and shotgun blast—a Gangster Queen.

But when I look at her, I still recall a frightened school girl lying under a wanna-be gangster in the dim light of a musty garage, lost amidst a sea of dusty beige. I see wide eyes trusting me when I whisper, "Don't worry, I got you."

BLACKBURN'S
Douglas S.

I remember long ago, living in Santa Paula, going to the fourth grade. All young, happy students would walk to school down Savior Road past Echo Park, past a store called Blackburn's.

It was in Blackburn's store that I saw a display of toys that spun around. On that display were some compasses—the kind you used to draw circles with.

I had what I thought was a great idea. I would hold my arm up alongside the display, letting the sleeve of my jacket open up, right under the treasured compasses. As I raised my arm, my sleeve would swallow the compass, lift it off its hook, allowing it to fall down my sleeve. I would then grab the toy above the compass, examine it, and decide not to buy the toy, walking out of Blackburn's with a free compass. That was my first day of crime.

JOEY
Jose C.

I grew up believing that the people who say they love you will be the ones to hurt you. I couldn't trust people. My dad left us when I was three, which led to my mom leaving me with my grandma. That didn't last long though. I was around 6 when my grandma died, and I moved back in with my mom. She was devastated by the death and did what most people do and resorted to alcohol. Living with her was especially bad for me, because I looked like my dad—the person who cheated on her and took her youth. During some of the beatings I wondered where some of the objects came from. One time I got hit with a hubcap.

By the time I was 10, I found myself in a foster home—both parents in jail, dad doing life, moms just a month. During my time in the system, I felt numb, unworthy, and abandoned. I promised myself no one would hurt or leave me again. I would be the one hurting and leaving.

So, when my Uncle Martin got me out of the foster home, I was no longer Joey. I went to my room, unpacked nothing, laid down and pondered my options. At 13 I had given up on myself. I was in a gang, selling drugs, and committing crimes. I overheard my Aunt Martha say, "He's just like his dad." She was right.

But today, I am almost done serving my 17-year sentence. Today, Joe is loving, trusting, and happy, thanks to Jesus Christ. He restored all my relationships, and He restored me. With God, I will never be abandoned again.

I DON'T CARE
Brian L.

"I don't care." Simple words expressing absence of an opinion. But for me, they became a protective mantra. I used "I don't care" to hide my emotions. "I don't care" seemed innocent enough at the time, but after a while, they would swallow me whole.

I used the words when I didn't want to accept the shame of an alcoholic household. They protected me from the sting of ridicule for shopping at thrift stores for clothes. When I began to fail in school, they shielded my pride.

"I don't care" insulated my heart from pain the first time it was broken. The words replaced tears and sadness with apathy, even cruelty. Eventually, I would trade my compassion and humanity for the perceived power, strength, and courage of indifference. When I found others who, like me, didn't care, our collective "I don't care" enabled us to commit acts of violent insanity.

As the years passed, "I don't care" ate at me. Like an emotional cancer, it infected all that I might have become. Those words echoed in the hollowness of my heart. Failures had no effect; loneliness meant nothing; love, even less. Ultimately, life itself lost value. "I don't care" had replaced everything.

Those words became the only truth in a universe without meaning or hope. "I don't care" led me to prison for life; and as I received a life-without-possibility-of-parole sentence in court, "I don't care" whispered its empty comfort to me.

Many, many years later, the "I-don't-cares" were silenced. One day, a new voice, full of hope and love, whispered to me. A spark of hope, in the hellish darkness of my soul, seemed as bright as a super nova. "I don't care" was transformed. It no longer represented an apathy about life, but a hopeful freedom. The words that once covered over pain and torment now enable acceptance and love. Even though I am sentenced to life, "I don't care." My spirit is free, and that's all that matters.

NOT ME!
Mario M.

My sixth grade teacher called on us at random, asking, "What do you want to be when you grow up?" Some students said a police officer, others a doctor, but not Laura, the teacher's pet. She said she wanted to be a lawyer, and I believed her. If they had let her, she would have brought a brief case to school. "Not me!" I thought to myself. All I wanted was the violence to stop in my house. But when the teacher called on me, I said the first thing that came to mind: a football player. I was too scared to tell the truth.

The bell rang, school was over. Most of the kids got excited and ran to the front of the school to get on the bus or get picked up. Not me! I hated to hear that bell ring: it meant I had to go home. I would walk to the back of the school to the last class room and sit on the wooden stairs until Dick, the janitor, worked his way back and kicked me out. He always said, "Son, you have to go home." That's when I'd start to ask him questions. Eventually, I knew everything about his job. Too bad I ran out of questions. After that, when I saw him rolling up with his cart, I would just leave.

One day I thought the violence was over. I opened the door to my house, and the first person I saw was my mom. She was in the kitchen crying. She looked scared and nervous, like her world was falling apart. Instead of getting scared with her, I felt a fire in my stomach. I already knew my dad had hit her. But this time, I told myself, I would not let him hit her anymore.

As I thought this, my dad reached over me and struck my mom in the face. I turned and kicked him in the leg. He tried again, and I punched him in the stomach. He began to slap me, but I kept after him. Finally, we both stopped. He looked at me and said, "She's my wife. It's none of your business." I told him, "It *is* my business; she's my mother." He glared at me, "You are no longer my son." And he left.

I felt really happy, my mind racing towards all the things I was going to accomplish, now that my father was gone. I didn't even know where to start. I didn't care; things were going to be different.

At school the next day, I moved from the back to the front of the class. I found a seat next to Laura Aguilar. She was surprised, but gave me a big smile. I asked her for help on our history assignment. She said, "Okay, start by re-reading your paper." I can still remember her writing, "messy."

The bell rings. School is over. I run home. As I turn the corner, I notice my dad's truck parked out front. My world comes crashing down. I open the front door and see my parents fighting. I couldn't believe she let him back in.

CRYSTAL BOX
Ricardo G.

Many years ago there was a five-year-old boy with dreams of one day becoming an architect, so that he could build a pretty house for his mom. The little boy also had a great hope of one day being able to erase his mother's pain and provide her with everlasting happiness.

On any given day, the little boy's mother would suddenly start cursing God for all of her problems and the miserable circumstances of her life. She would start screaming profanities and breaking things around the house. The little boy began to feel panic and anxiety every time he saw his mother act this way. He could sense her desperation. The little boy didn't know what to do to help his mother.

One day the little boy got a pencil and a piece of paper and drew a pretty house for his mother. He presented it to her and with a soft voice and an innocent smile, he said, "I promise you that when I grow up I will build a pretty house for you, Mom, so you won't have to work anymore." The mother caressed her son's head, gave him a kiss on his forehead and told him that she loved him, that she was very proud for having such a good and loving son. For a moment, the little boy felt like a superhero. He felt so happy and proud for putting his mother in a good mood, at least momentarily.

The little boy continued to dream of one day becoming an architect until violence and trauma began to crush his dreams. Without warning, the little boy's father would come home drunk and beat up the little boy's mother. Her misery would return along with her bad mood. The little boy would again try to bring a smile to her face and put her in a happy mood by sharing his dreams and hopes with her.

For a while, this was enough to console his mom, but eventually she refused to be consoled. She began to take her anger and frustration out on the little boy. The little boy was sad and afraid. He didn't know how to deal with it.

Then one day, I appeared in the little boy's life. In an effort to protect him I took him under my wing. I gently put him in a crystal box. I laid a foundation of fear, disappointment, disillusionment, and indifference. Then I began to build the walls, one rock at a time:

rocks of anger, resentment, selfishness, malice—and many, many more heavy and ugly rocks.

The little boy with big dreams and great hopes was helpless and hopeless. Initially, he complained. He told me he didn't like the thought of being isolated from the rest of the world. He begged me many times to please let him out, especially when his parents realized the damage they had inflicted on him. Although the wall around us was very high, we could still hear the people calling to us from the outside. But I refused to let anybody in.

The little boy's mother was persistent and asked for his forgiveness many times, but I always refused to grant it. The little boy asked, "Why not?" I replied, "We can't trust anyone." I justified my poor choices and bad decisions by holding on to my resentments and insisting that he needed to be protected from the bad people in the world. "Don't worry." I would say. "I'll never let anybody hurt you."

One day the little boy stopped asking questions. In fact, he stopped talking all together, and I became oblivious to his presence. With the little boy thrown into oblivion, I roamed alone, trapped behind the ugly wall I had built. After years of loneliness and self-destruction, I finally pulled the little boy from his crystal box. He was weak and malnourished, but still alive. Thank you, God!

I held the little boy in my arms. The look in his eyes made my heart ache. I spoke to him for the first time in many years. I asked, "Why did you stop talking to me, little boy?" He answered, "I never did. It was you who stopped listening." He didn't condemn, didn't reprehend, didn't criticize or blame me for anything. He just asked me in a very soft and calm voice that broke my heart, "What happened to my hopes and dreams?"

The little boy gave me a lesson in courage, humility, and forgiveness. He didn't cry when he saw the tears in my eyes. He reached out with his little hands to wipe them away, then gave me a reassuring smile and said, "Don't worry. Everything's going to be alright. I forgive you for everything you've wronged. I always knew your intentions were good, though your means were wrong. Even though you've ignored me, I never stopped worrying about you. I love you and I want you to learn how to forgive. Would you please let me help you?"

How could I say no to the little boy? I'd hurt him so much and yet he showed me nothing but love. I began to listen to him and together we started to tear down my ugly wall. Finally, we're venturing back into the world. I know there are going to be times when I am going to be hurt and afraid, but that's when I have to remember the little boy has shown me: love overcomes pain, fear, and anything else.

I know that as he grows stronger, the little boy will eventually take control of our life. Perhaps one day he will write another chapter to this story. As for me, he's become my daily inspiration. His willingness to love and forgive, to help and understand, and his amazing ability for compassion are some of the characteristics and traits that I want to learn and imitate. Today, I can say with confidence that you were right, little boy. Everything's going to be all right.

FRIENDS
Johnny S.

The "Pearl of the South Pacific" bred three young boys who ran barefoot through the lush green grass of Samoa. Their vestures were nothing but an Ie Lava Lava (a traditional garment tied loosely around the waist). We ran with joy and laughter through the tall grass and into the dark green jungle toward the ocean. The day was beautiful and sunny. It was great to get away from chores for a day of swimming and spear fishing in the ocean we so loved.

The jungle holds both hidden treasures and dangers. Each boy carried a homemade slingshot for protection. Dangerous animals lurked everywhere.

We walked without care, pretending we weren't scared. We laughed and enjoyed the sweet taste of freshly picked mango and papaya. Following behind us were my nameless dogs. Their playful scampering told me that they, too, were excited about the trip.

When we stopped momentarily to rest, I could hear the jungle talking, especially the little noises of small animals when they, too, heard something unfamiliar. Birds chirped back and forth and flapped their way to safety. An owl hooted an unknown message—so scary, yet so beautiful and peaceful.

Stepping out into the clearing and seeing the ocean was exciting: clear, blue water as far as my eyes could see. I felt like I was standing at the very end of the world.

Using our slingshots to hunt for food, we roasted birds over an open fire and drank coconut juice.

Suddenly, we heard the sound of a big angry animal, tree branches cracking under its hooves. My heart was pounding out of my chest. I wanted to run, but dared not show any fear in front of my friends. A big, ugly wild pig lurched into the open. Seeing my brother's fearful reaction, I dropped my slingshot and ran to the nearest tree, followed by my friends, and climbed to safety. We had great adventures, which led those three boys from the island to grow up to live different lives.

Strings removed from an old Ie Lava Lava are now sown into the fabric of my visiting clothes, linking me forever to my lost paradise. The state added leg irons and waste chains—custom jewelry to break hearts.

Walking into the visiting room, she mused at my jewelry. "Looks good on you," she laughed. And I smiled. I knew at that moment she would always be someone special in my life. This boy grew up to find the same sparkle of the South Pacific in the eyes of his beautiful wife

Violet:
Alofa ia te oe
Spoken softly
When every syllable counts
Words constructed by emotions
Make this heart melt
Alofa ia te oe
A lifetime taken
To finally admit it
Confessing my emotions
So glad that you're with it
Alofa ia te oe
My hard life disappears
Whenever our fingertips touch
Bonded together by commitment
I love you so much
Alofa ia te oe.....

BOOT CAMP
Bradley F.

I flew in on a Boeing 737 with 34 others. When the plane hit the ground, there were drill sergeants everywhere. One came onto the plane, barking orders, "You maggots have 60 seconds to get off this plane, and don't be last. Now, move!"

All at once, 35 grunts scrambled over seats and each other, making sure he was not last. Hitting the tarmac, we were hustled onto a bus and driven to Fort McClennan, deep in Alabama. I was thrown into a barber's chair and in less than 30 seconds, hairless. They took my Levi 501's and gave me cami-greens.

The next eight weeks were hell—physical training at 4:30 every morning, push ups, sit ups, a 3-to-5 mile run, then crawling in the mud under barbed wire and live gun fire. You liked it, you loved it, and you craved more.

Graduation day! I looked out the window to see everyone else's family, but not mine. Feeling like a child, I called my granny. "They didn't make it. They didn't come." She responded with what I needed to hear. "I'm so proud of you, I love you, go graduate. I'll take care of them when they get home."

I got to formation just as the senior drill sergeant yelled, "Fall in!" Hurting at the sight of everyone else's family, I dropped my head for a second. As I raised my eyes, I saw her. Damn, they made it! They came. My family.

PLANTING FLAGS
Tam N.

When I was six, I dreamt of walking on the moon and planting a huge "Tam was here" flag, so that everyone in the universe would know how great I was. I wanted to fly through space, bright white stars streaking by me. I'd explore exotic new worlds with purple skies, boiling green oceans full of life, and humanoid aliens with green skin who'd greet me as a hero for slaying their evil oppressors.

Sadly, my mother was a realist. She explained that an astronaut didn't conquer worlds and that aliens didn't exist. She did, however, encourage me to study math so that one day I might become a real astronaut and plant my flag. Learning that math is a pre-requisite to becoming an astronaut weakened my tiny, six-year-old resolve. To this day, every time I see an equation, my brain seizes. Math is my kryptonite. But my mother encouraged my childish dreams; so, I tried to learn.

When my parents' fighting became an everyday occurrence, she left. My world shattered: I could never be happy and innocent again. I didn't care about flying anymore. I didn't care about anything.

It took decades, but I finally found something that revived my childhood dream of leaving Earth. The guitar. Though I work on my feet all day, attend church studies, and self-help groups that require tons of homework, I make time to practice. I study Clapton, B. B. King, and Albert King, as well as other greats, copying every sound they make.

When my hand glides through a song, my lead and rhythm harmonizing perfectly, I'm soaring through space at the speed of light, the blazing, bright stars blinding me, and I'm loving it. For a brief moment, I'm in heaven. No more pain, no more regrets. Nothing else matters.

I'm working on becoming the best blues-rock guitarist I can be. When I feel I'm good enough and have written enough songs, I'll invest in a cell-phone, then put myself on YouTube, hoping that millions will love my music and write to me.

These days, I dream my guitar will take me to the moon: I can still plant my flag.

REASONS WHY
Patrick A.

I am hardly more than a toddler. "Quit crying. Suck it up!" My father shakes my boney shoulders, causing my brown bangs to hang over teary brow. He insists, "You've no reason to cry. Only sissies cry!" Lower lip quivers against baby teeth, holding my breath, as heaving lungs swallow tears...never to cry again. Not when shot and left for dead or abandoned to crowded juvenile hall, where children's blanketed sobs, betrayed by shuddering shoulders, lay strewn upon night-lit floors.

My dresser mirror frames my nineteen years, while invisible red ants violently snap chunks of constricted, chest-jerking throat, and glossy-teared eyes shout at mirrored self.

"We don't cry," my father mentally echoes, demanding control, like fifteen years ago. Looming tsunami threatens stony reform school stare, barricaded behind flimsy bedroom door, breeching emotional retaining wall, fortified since age four.

Hunched puny before black, watery wall, flushed cheeks touch fuchsia, as white-fisted knuckles pound brown dresser, "You sissy-ass punk!" Condemning tears sear my skin purple. "Suck it up," more plea than demand, "You've no reason to..." Nerves break, as child's boney shoulders surface above sorrow's murky abyss to wrestle control beneath teary depths—down and down 'til drowned; swept away by 15 million reasons why.

THAT LITTLE BOY
Oscar R.

December 5, 1978. Leaving my safe haven, I was cursed into existence, narrowly escaping death. Tumbling down a staircase of a blazing apartment, my mother was rushed to a hospital. She claims an angel of man broke her fall, possibly saving her life, certainly saving mine. The good Samaritan's name was Oscar, hence my name—doubly cursed!

She found herself in that death trap of an apartment because her abusive husband, drunk as usual, was beating her, forcing her to flee into the night with children in tow. She could've risked staying home, praying the alcohol would become her ally, putting father to sleep. Or she could chance spending the night in her car, parked on the murderous streets of West Los Angeles. Fearing for her children's safety, mom chose the condemned apartment as her refuge.

As a young boy, I wondered at the grimness of my situation, being tossed to and fro by vicious winds of misfortune; smacked about by ferocious thirty-foot waves of hatred; submerged in waters so cold they made the fires of hell seem merciful. I was born into a perfect storm that never ceased. With a fight-or-flight mechanism permanently activated, I didn't know what it was to feel normal—childhood abandoning me as I cower in the trenches of my mind, detaching myself from the idea of love.

My father hated life and made his family follow him down the path of misery. He had a special hate reserved for me, accusing my skin color of betrayal. Viewed through the eyes of Mexican machismo, I looked too white to be his son. Never feeling the warmth of a loving father or the nurturing embrace of a loving mother (he wouldn't let her), I ran to the outstretched arms of the street.

I fit right into a life of crime, eagerly dishing out the same punishment that had been inflicted on me. Soon enough, I found myself in prison, Satan's breeding ground. My first instinct promised nothing good from this place, and I believed it, feeling the ugliness surround me and not yet knowing that in all things, God works for good with those who love Him, those who he has called according to his purpose.

God helped me shed those thick layers of hate that blinded me from His love. Each layer he peeled off was a slow, excruciating death, torturing me with thoughts of, "What if there is worse ugliness underneath?" I dreaded finding father's reason for hating me.

When God finished, he unwrapped the bandages, revealing something I had lost so long ago. I finally met that little boy, his heart so full of joy, begging me to let him play. His laughter echoes in my mind, as I recall his first tickle party only a few weeks ago—and a wife and daughter amazed at the innocent laughter of a thirty-three year old boy.

LITTLE ME, BIG ME
Michael M.

Osh Kosh B'gosh clothing was awesome; now prison blues are the rage. Clowns, both big and small, made me laugh; now I'm surrounded by them. Girlfriends had cooties; now I'd do anything for one. Pizza cost me nothing; now I can't even buy one. Television was for videogames; now it's for seeing the outside. Friends were always there for me; now they're hit and miss. What happened to me? Where did I go wrong?

RESURRECTION
Julian V.

A child and his innocence die at five: confusion and horror begin. "Boy come here. Do you see that closet? The Boogeyman lives in there, and if I let him out, he will eat you! Do what I say and you will be safe, and I will give you some candy. Now, take off your pants." A lost and confused little soul did what he was told.

Tears passed as the years turned gray. He empowered himself with violence, anger, and hate. Thinking he was all grown up at ten, he joined a gang, did drugs, drank, and had sex. He never thought back to the day the horror show began. This li'l man, no longer ten, is now grown—and in prison.

A bearded man came to him in a dream. The man was of medium build, kind of tall, brown hair to the shoulders and dressed all in white, radiating light all around him. There was peace about him. We both stood in an open plane with golden grass swaying on a gentle breeze. To one side was an ancient oak with 12 large branches.

I looked up to the man as he smiled at me, and I smiled back. I heard a giggle, then more giggles. They were coming from behind him, from a li'l fat kid. The boy moved shyly from behind the man. I looked closely: he looked so familiar. I extended my hand and the boy took it. I woke up and went to the mirror. There I saw the child within.

WOULD LIFE BE DIFFERENT?
Robert G.

My parents were addicts. I was "at risk," as they say, from birth. They went to prison and custody of my siblings and me went to our 19-year-old aunt. A single parent, she would now be caring for nine children, one with a heart condition. The stress of her life led her to heroin addiction.

I was two when my mother got out, and I was returned to her care. When I was five, an older sister and brother started getting me high on marijuana. My sister thought it was funny. I started stealing taffy candy from Banner's Market until my sister caught me and made me tell the owner, Bill. He humiliated me by writing it on a chalkboard for everybody to see: I, Robert G., stole from his store.

I ran away just before turning nine. When I returned two weeks later, Mom told me she hadn't come looking for me because she knew where I was the whole time. That told me I had to find family elsewhere.

Feeling abandoned and worthless, I sought acceptance and love in the alleyways, getting jumped in to a Los Angeles street gang at ten. My brother's homeboys were now mine, as well.

I continued to feel hurt and anger. I started carrying a gun and selling drugs, as I sought recognition and status. I became extremely aggressive and by 15, I had managed three assault convictions. Just after my 16th birthday, I was facing multiple life sentences.

At 17, I opened Calipatria State Prison, considered then to be the most violent prison in California. A boy amongst men, I felt I had to prove my toughness. I met and became friends with a man named Sal there, the man we now know as "The Mooch," a man who I would know for many years—and prisons.

I had led a violent, dangerous, and destructive lifestyle; but God's mercy kept me alive, healthy, and helped me avoid turning my "life with the possibility of parole" sentence into "life without" or even my own death.

Would life be different if I wasn't born addicted, hadn't spent 23 years incarcerated, or hadn't met Sal 22 years ago—angry, selfish, and unforgiving? Perhaps, without all of that, I wouldn't be as grateful today. I am thankful "The Mooch" gave me this opportunity—

through C.G.A., re-entry, and this class—to learn, to change and to share with others, the man I have worked to become—humble, caring and kind.

JARHEAD AT HEART
Brett T.

I was only five when Frank, my oldest brother, left for boot camp. I was so young and scared that my brother was leaving and that I wasn't gonna see him again, that I wouldn't let go. We had played cowboys and Indians, cops and robbers, and best of all, GI Joe. I would miss my brother.

Three weeks later, he woke me up by jumping on me. We started wrestling around, and it was great. I was happy, but I could see a sadness I didn't understand at five. Frank was kicked out of boot camp. It killed him inside.

The reason? Frank and his best friend Danny were in a nasty car wreck almost a year earlier. Danny swerved to make an off ramp. The car flipped on its side, pinning my brother's arm and, as the car slid over 100 feet, ripping his arm to pieces. I remember the doctor saying the only reason he still had his arm was the three-inch wide leather watch-band he wore. They did skin grafts from his thigh to his arm. I thought it was so ugly to look at.

After Frank came home, he went crazy! To me, I was just playing with my brother. But he started doing push-ups, jumping jacks, running... I loved it! A seed was planted, and I was gonna be a Marine like my big brother. I was being groomed to be a jarhead, my walls and door covered with, "The Few, The Proud, The Marines."

For ten years, all I wanted was to follow my brother. He climbed the ranks fast while I started getting into drugs, running the streets, and stealing cars. One night, in a deep depression, I did a shot of speed, then went out and robbed and killed someone. And all my hopes and dreams faded.

Frank went on to retire as a one-star general. He lives here in San Diego, but we haven't spoken since 1985. I guess we both had expectations of each other, and I let him down. He still can't handle what I did to my family.

But I have new hopes and dreams: to go home, to be a good husband to my wife, father to my grown kids, grandpa to my grandkids, and to give back to society the best I can. Ultimately, my biggest hope is to be a better person, with each passing day.

THE RED MAHOGANY DOOR
Jojo D.

In the roach-infested motel, home to Rampart District hookers and crack heads, I wake screaming in a feverish sweat. My father's condemning eyes burn my soul. His image, a remnant of a recurring nightmare, hauntingly fades to blackness. Far in the corner, my twin brother sits in a cheap, vinyl chair, dimly lit by a small table lamp. With knowing eyes, he slowly rises to hand me the death stick he'd been pulling—our last—and we exit the gloomy room.

At 3am, with a cool breeze swaying on the motel balcony, boulders of sweat fall to an empty parking lot, drying my skin tight, the only sound, a neon sign buzzing "Vacancy"—buzz, buzz... silence. My mind reels as I relive my nightmare of that fateful day. My father shouted, "I hate you, you worthless, drugged out thug! Bahala Mo, Layas! Get the hell out and don't ever show your face again. You're dead to me."

It had been a week since we'd left home—a week of meth and dumpster diving behind McDonald's. But it couldn't keep me from missing my mom. The translucent cord of the phone coiled around my fist like a viper when my mother, voice fueled by anger, screamed to me through the receiver, "I'll call the police!" In the next breath, sobs of life draining out of her, she begged, "Please come home..." Her words ripped my heart. Tears in my eyes, I ripped the phone from the wall and launched it across the room.

Coming home, standing outside the red mahogany door of my father's house, thoughts crashed wildly in my head, his words still haunting me. "I can't do it, I can't face him. I can't go home."

Time froze. I knew he was right, every harsh word true. Stepping inside, heart pounding with fear, the mahogany door shuts behind me.

NOURISHING ANGER
Tam N.

It was the filthiest place I'd ever seen. The grey walls of the cell were carved with the gang initials and nicknames of those who'd been here before. Red and brown smears of blood and shit stained the walls and parts of the floor. The smell of piss and sweat burned my nostrils.

A long slab of concrete, connecting to opposing walls, served as my bed. It was like a huge hunk of ice that seeped the night's frost into the cell. In search of warmth, I had to lie in a ball while breathing into cupped hands with a blanket pulled tightly over my head.

Shivering, I lay there pondering how my life got so screwed up. I was only 14. I'd been living in stolen cars, sometimes selling them to crack-heads for money to eat. Who lived like this? Why didn't anyone care about me?

I remember the police laughing at me when I told them I had no one to call to pick me up. "Worthless nip" they smirked, just before one of them entered to rough me up. I fought to hold back tears. They were right. I was worthless. Not even my family gave a shit about me. "Fuck the police! Fuck my family! Fuck this world!"

Being angry kept me from falling apart. Rage sustained me.

THE CULMINATION
Brian L.

I was nauseated for most of that morning, as much from nerves as from starving myself to make my weight limit. It had been an exhausting day of physical exams, standing around in my underwear with the fluorescent lights above and ice-cold linoleum below. No matter how embarrassing the process, I kept thinking "It's all worth it."

Bored, I let my mind drift back to when the whole neighborhood would gather in the open fields. I would dress in my fatigue pants and t-shirt, and we'd divide into teams. We would run and hide, using sticks as rifles and fingers for guns. Each weekend, battles were fought and wars were waged, as we staged ambushes and scouted for enemies. We had highly advanced tactics for such a motley crew of kids.

I snapped back to reality, and put my clothes back on. Finally, my turn came to sit with a staff sergeant and discuss my future. He handed me a book with all the possible careers to choose from. As I slowly scanned the different descriptions and possibilities, I felt the strings of my past loosen. I got a sense of destiny and freedom I had never known. The last eighteen years fell away, and I could see that I had made it.

As a child, I had lived for mornings, with a diet of crunchy cereal, TV, movies, toys, and cartoons, all driving an idea to be like one of them—a soldier. Now, the dream was coming true.

Back to reality again: I chose a career and signed a contract. Not many would be so thrilled to give their life away, but that was not me. I was jumping for joy. I was sent to another room, this one different from the others.

It was warm with sunlight. I realized it had been a long day, and took a seat with the other recruits. The US flag covered the wall behind a podium; a strange buzz of anticipation filled the room. Each of us whispered the same questions, "What'd you get? Where are you going?" Each hopeful to find a buddy.

Suddenly, the room went still, and a sergeant told us to stand. A captain entered, uniform full of patches and symbols, with brass and silver gleaming in the sunlight, none of which I understood, but wanted more than my first kiss. We raised our right hands and repeated after him. The large flag and shining buttons and embroidered patches mesmerized me. I became hyper-aware of each second, as time almost stopped, my heart pounding furiously in my chest. A cold sweat broke out. I stated my name. I recited the oaths, grinning from ear to ear. As I said the words, my mind screamed, "I did it, I did it!"

When we were done, the captain's words brought it all together, "You're in the Army."

PART 2. PAIN

Make the most of your regrets; never smother your sorrow, but tend and cherish it till it comes to have a separate and integral interest. To regret deeply is to live afresh.

- Henry David Thoreau

NOBODY'S FAULT BUT MINE
Bradley F.

Time heals all wounds, but can't erase the scars. I was fourteen years old when Mari moved next door. She was a year older; the Puerto Rican Princess with raven-colored hair, caramel complexion, and green eyes had my heart from the second I saw her. For months, she toyed with me as if I was her personal play thing. On my fifteenth birthday, she laid down the rules: "Don't lie to me, don't cheat on me, and I will always be yours." Best birthday ever!

The rules changed when we had our first child. At 21, I called her every bluff by not coming home for days, cheating, and lying to her face. Yet she stayed—through military, three trials, and sixteen years of this life sentence, hiding the hurt, pain, and frustration I caused.

Feeling her hands tremble as I held them, I could barely hear her say, "I can't do this anymore. I can't be this close to you and not be with you. If you really love me, you have to let me go." At that moment, I felt my heart break. I still wear the ugly scar and it's nobody's fault but mine.

ON THE OTHER SIDE OF PAIN
Dontay T.

The sound of shattering picture frames filled my ears, as they ripped past my head, crashing violently against the living room wall. "Who the hell is she, Don-Tay!?" "Angela, ma, please calm down." Smash! A porcelain lamp disintegrated at my feet. "I don't wanna hear that shit! Who is she!?" The sight of mascara running down her honeysuckle cheeks tormented my soul. I never meant to hurt Angela, nor was I willing to sever our relationship. Yesterday, we had one of our famous lovers' quarrels, and I decided to give her some space by having a guys' night out with the fellas. We decided to catch Mike Capps live downtown, doing stand up comedy at the House of Blues.

The reddish glow of neon lamps complemented each table, while thick purple smoke radiated through the air, sending mellow vibes throughout the club. A glittering display of royal jewels flickered from underneath my black and gray Louis Vutton jacket, as we entered the V.I.P. lounge. The blend of Brandy and French Cognac had a smooth but passionate kick, as it intoxicated my mind, causing me to reminisce about the adorable 5-foot-3-inch Puerto Rican-Filipino queen I left at home. I felt incomplete without her.

Angela and I had been through hell and back, and there was nothing I wouldn't do for her. I remember the first time I laid eyes on her. It was at Plaza Bonita mall in an urban store called Shieks. If I wasn't obnoxiously conceited with a pocket full of green ego, I would have easily turned into a puddle of drool. Instead, I walked up to her, picked up golden lace Prada Stilettos, and sighed loud enough for her to hear, before theatrically musing, "Only an angel could pull these off". I turned and smiled, causing her to blush and bashfully smile back.

Now, I'm left with only pain, having to look into her eyes and explain why and how the smudges of lipstick got on my collar, and the fragrance that she never sprays.

LOVE IS PAIN
Manuel R.

When I saw her, my heart melted. I couldn't speak, dumb founded by her beauty. Lost in her eyes, I saw my soul flying free. Dark brown curls covered her peach-skin face, big red lips softer and sweeter than angel's candy. My Puerto Rican-Portuguese goddess became my life force of love and mother of our two proudest achievements, made from pure love. Falling asleep in each others' arms, "God made us for each other," she would whisper in my ear. Watching love bounce from our four-month old baby boy on lap, I fell to my knees, grabbing her hand. "You mean the world to me and I could never love another. You gave me two beautiful boys. You three give me a reason to live and love. I want us to grow old together, like our grandparents with our grandchildren around us. Will you marry me?"

Placing ring on finger, a kiss and hug that still send tears down my face. Love is Forever...."Bang! Bang!" The voices at the door call throughout the house. "Freeze! On the ground! Now!" they yell. A scream that haunts me day and night, "NO, NO, NO!" she cries "NO, you can't take him! Babe, NOOOO!"

Looking down, I see a scared little angel's arms stretched toward me, begging me to pick him up. "I can't, mijo. Love you, my big boy."

Seventeen years later, her screams still tear at me. Heartbroken, I know I lost my life force and destroyed our family. I dread sunsets, knowing sleep follows night. The pain of dreaming comes and goes. The whisper of "God made us for each other" is lost in distant love, turned now to a life of the pain I caused.

BETRAYAL
Craig H.

"Why are you pushing me away?" she asked over and over through the inch thick visiting window of the Orange County Men's Jail. Unresponsive and broken by reality, shackled by waist chains and leg irons, I gave a distant stare. Her tears broke my silence. I forced the tight chain up my chest allowing me to reach the phone. "I never meant to hurt you," my voice cracked—a statement made with regret, as I watched her pain give way to anger.

Displaying her left hand, I saw the promise ring with the engraved words "Never shall I abandon you." I'd given it to her years ago. Taking a deep breath and shutting my eyes, I dropped my head in shame, tapping into emotions I had attempted to bury. The dagger of guilt finally pierced my heart.

CRIES OF DESPAIR
Kevin H.

Pitter-pattering feet tap across the laminate floor, arms stretched wide, smiles ear to ear, eyes locked onto me as a pilot to her target. She sought me out of the gloom with screams of "Daddy! Daddy! Daddy!" penetrating to the very core of my soul.

As I exited the hardness of prison walls to the softness of innocent love, chubby-cheeked Ashleigh Nicole would draw me into a world of unfamiliarity with charges like, "Daddy, when are you getting out?" and "Please, play with me."

She turned prison warrior into mushy clown, teaching me patty cake while her laughter bellowed from her little belly. Fifty-two card pickup and jumps from the slide into my arms were her favorites. This was a love I'd forever cling to.

Institutional figures, however, had a different view. Four more years was the proclamation. Her mother could no longer fathom this horrific scene. Visits diminished, and Ashleigh was torn, unawares, from my grasp. Love was lost and Ashleigh gone. I spiraled into cries of despair, fading memories of Ash, heart scourged by her innocent love.

THEN AND NOW
Dino J.

Radiant she glows calling within
Seducing my senses with her lingering charms
Memories of love, cherished and true
Summoned to remind me, in darkness shines hope
A flickering flame to extinguish my hate
Warmth now shining to all seclusions
Near and far
Though ages have passed, and my one
Has moved on
I still dream of what was
In a smile for today

PART 3. PARENTHOOD

Children make you want to start life over.

- Muhammad Ali

PRIDE AND JOY
Brett T.

"Babes, wake up! My water broke!" It's the morning of May 10, 1974. Dazed, I jump up, grab my car keys, her suitcase, and rush out the door.

Racing to Children's Hospital at 1:00am, running red lights all the way, we scream into emergency parking. Out comes a wheel chair and off she goes. I pace up and down the hall waiting to hear something...anything!

It took six hard hours of labor before Joshua Paul popped into the world. Moms and I stood in front of the window looking at the little bundle with my name on it. My mom looked at me and said, "You did a good job." Being a 14 year old kid, I said, "I did a good job 9 months ago!" She slapped me hard, yelling, "You're a baby having a baby!" In shock, I stared at my pride and joy, my one and only boy. Mom was right. I was a baby having a baby.

MISSING OUT
Nicholas F.

The crowd cheers as a young, lanky girl, hair tied back, hustles to the plate. CRACK!! The bat connects with the ball, sending it blazing back to the pitcher. The natural-born athlete catches the ball, throwing the runner out at first. High fives all around, as they win the little league championship. High school, game on the line, she fires a screaming pitch: "Strike three!" College scouts take notice as she wins her high school championship. Criminal Justice major playing third base in cactus country, she does well in college, still a skilled athlete with a cannon arm.

"Bang, bang, bang!" knocks me back to reality, "Last two", barks the guard at my door. Looking at the walls of my cage, pictures of my beautiful baby girl who has grown into a lovely young lady—the life I missed. What if I had not followed my older brother around the streets of Los Angeles, terrorizing our community? I would have been there to raise my daughter. What if I had not pulled that gun from my waistband and ended Frank's life? What if I had not chosen gang life over taking care my baby girl, being the father she deserved? I would have been in Arizona, cheering her on at third.

FOOL, I DO!
Melvin P.

Why does your hair look like that? Why aren't white people black, and why won't my boomerang fly back? Why should I be scared of black cats? And, where all the Indians like in the movies at?

What came first, the chicken or the egg? I bet you don't know how Beyonce got those legs. Who invented A.I.D.S., and what about Nike's?

With all the things in the ocean that want to eat you, who was the first person that thought it was a good idea to swim in the sea?

What would happen if the moon was made of cheese?

Why did Christopher Columbus sail all the way across the ocean for some salt? If we live in the "United States," why are some things legal in some states, but against the law in others? Don't sound very united to me.

What's the capital of Singapore? What's the first thing you would do if they let you go home tomorrow?

How much wood could a woodchuck chuck? What does it mean to be "shit out of luck"? How can I watch my mouth? Who would win a bar fight, Miley Cyrus or Justin Bieber? Do only people living in the jungle catch jungle fever? If people live in a place called The Projects, does that mean someone is experimenting on them? Why can't homeless people live in the White House? School teaches us the White House belongs to the citizens of the U.S.A., so why can't you have a felony and go inside you own house?

My thirteen-year-old son Nile, who introduces himself, "Hi, my name is Nile, like the river, with no 's'," is smart. He enjoys proving me wrong. His favorite phrase is "Why Not"? I recently encouraged him to say, "There's no such thing as a bad question." Big Mistake!

The moral of this story is, never get into an argument with your thirteen-year-old son, and when he exclaims, "You think you know everything, don't you!" Respond with "Fool, I Do!"

MY SON
Tyrone H.

Mighty as the Great Mississippi they flow, streaking aimlessly down my face. Passion-filled and relentless, my tears journey downward, picking up speed at the curve of my nose. Despite the brush of a heavy hand, they continue on.

Thoughts of my son evoke pain and regret, turning often to tears. Forced to live a fatherless childhood because of my irresponsible decisions and behavior, my son was left wondering what he could possibly have done to make his father choose prison over him.

Each tear, burning its own trail down my face, speaks of the pain suffocating my heart and the horror of my decisions. Seeking not the removal of my tears, only the renewal of a relations with my child, I wish only a chance to be...a father; to be there!

IT'S A SMILE TO ME!
Ramon G.

February, 1991. Jittery nerves, pounding heart—the wait was over. "Are you ready?" boomed the authoritative voice over the intercom. Door slides open. Trembling intensifies every step down the metal stairs. Peering faces from cell windows smile in reassurance. They know today is my day and understand my anxiety.

Two more sliding doors, no turning back. I walk inside the cold room, taking one of three metal stools. Elevator light flicks, announcing its arrival. Door opens: they step out.

Taking the seat in front of me, mother smiles. "Meet your daughter, Leticia."

Will she grow up ashamed of me? Will she hate me for depriving her of a real father? Will she even want me in her life? Wrestling with these thoughts, I look in amazement at this precious, innocent blessing peacefully resting in my mother's arms.

Then it happened. Opening her beautiful brown eyes, she greets me with a smile. Instantly, my fears and worries vanish.

Mother smiles, "Ay mijo, she just passed gas." "It's ok Ama, I'll take what I can get."

MEMORIES
Bradley F.

At two months, Shawn Tae knew she had me wrapped around her finger. She was my first child and will always be Daddy's Little Girl. Her laughter, mixed with the look in her eyes, oozed pure love. Holding her as I watched a Lakers game, tired eyes asleep on my chest, I dared not move.

Those memories warm my heart and keep me sane. Shuffled from cage to cage for 24 years, I embrace the joys of love—my distant past. Dragging the weight of rusty chains, feeling the wrath of those who despise me, I was belittled, cursed, and nearly forgotten. My pride stills my tears, as I warmly recall the love in my daughter's eyes. The joy of her laughter has kept me through the years.

And I smile.

PRECIOUS
Albert L.

The moment I saw your face, I finally understood true, genuine love. Listening to the strong beats of your little heart made me cry. Five fingers on each hand and five toes on each foot elicited prayers of "Thank you, God."

The way you gripped my thumb and didn't want to let it go told me, "a daddy's girl." The little ears and mouth made me think, "Sorry, you look like Daddy." The loud crying told me, "Oh no! You have a bit of Mommy too!" When you opened your eyes, I was reminded of a rare emerald. Your eyes pierced my soul. I laughed and cried at the same time.

"What good have you done to deserve such a precious gift?" When I laid you upon my war-scarred chest and inhaled the newness of life, I was filled with unexplainable feelings. I would do anything for you, my angel, even give up my life. The sound of your barely audible snores brought relief, teaching me I wasn't the only one now.

I settled down. Then you gave me a smile that made me lose it: I never cried so much in my life. In that moment I knew how precious life was and held tightly to all that it offers. The next time things are going downhill, I will remember that smile that said, "It's ok Daddy, I love you."

MY NAME IS
Johnny S.

My little girl's milky-white vomit covered my shoulder and slowly dripped down my back as her tiny arms waved up and down. As I cherished the memory of that short time spent with her, I wondered if I'd ever hold my daughter again. That was 32 years ago—before bad decisions landed me in a musty cage reserved for the living dead. And the years dragged by.

Four manila envelopes addressed by an unfamiliar hand recently stepped into my gated home. They contained nearly a hundred pictures of my seven grandkids—six handsome boys and a cute little girl, she in a grass skirt and pink slippers, hula dancing with the stars. They'd inherited their Grandpa Johnny's gorgeous looks, and it made me smile—a reflection of joy from deep within. I am proud to see that the vomit-spewing baby girl has grown into a beautiful woman with children of her own.

Tears of joy flowed freely as I read from the first of eight letters: "My name is Justin. I'm sixteen and I'm your oldest grandson."

CHEERS AND SOFT TEARS
Oscar M.

A legacy of hopes and dreams—and freedom! I close my eyes, open my heart, and dream of a very different me. Flying through space and time, I fast-forward the negative me, skipping over the hurt and screeching pain. I land as if from a plane smack into a human heart. I sense warmth, love, and admiration.

I hear the giggling sound of laughter in the midst of soft whispers of "I love you." I feel the hugs of genuine affection, cheers, and soft tears. I feel the constant tugging on my pant legs, as if by many tiny hands. I look to see with drowning tears. My heart smiles as it beats violently, not with fear but with something different—adoration!

I'm overwhelmed. I look down, my gaze falling deep into a dark well of piercing eyes. I am captured, hypnotized by innocence.

"Grampa! Grampa! Grampa!" The tugging little hand shouts. My heart laughs in disbelief, the pain of long ago vanquished. Love spews out from every pore. I am floating! Flying! What honor!

Many little hearts filled with dreams gather around the campfire of my heart. Hot embers of duty colorfully brighten my future. My grandchildren happily clothe me with commitment. My reinforced goodness leaps out of my hands. I must teach and nurture them. I dream of being a giant—morally tall and courageous enough to help them believe in themselves.

"You can do it! You can overcome! You have been made for many great things! Grampa will help you through the storm, the rain, and the shattering pain. Even when my hand becomes weak, I will help you stand tall."

I drop to one knee. I am tackled by hugs, hugs, and more hugs—a beautiful clinging sensation. Sparkling eyes and wide smiles with missing teeth speak musical notes of a warmth unknown.

Grampa has heard a divine whisper: you were once a child; now you have grown. Life has been harsh, but you did not fold. You have known well the disabling pain of solitude. Now you will find the healing touch of love. Heal and mend well, for you will live long and bright.

MI HERMOSA BEBE
Ricardo G.

Many years before you were born someone told me about the undeserved gift of love from God. "Amazing Grace" they called it. Someone told me God offers forgiveness for my sins even if society doesn't think I deserve it. Someone told me that God loves me despite my crimes.

I did not believe any of it. I always thought that if God really loved me, He would show his love for me somehow: how could His love be real when all I saw around me was misery and selfishness?

I was too angry at my parents for the misery they put me through as a child to see any love there. I was bitter with society; I never felt an expression of love from it. So I made things make sense for me: it was simple. My parents hurt me, so I hurt them. Society didn't care about me, so I didn't care about society. I saw no love, I felt no love, so I showed no love.

Then, you appeared in my life when I needed you the most. You spoke to me softly and tenderly, words that I never expected to hear. You said, "I love you and I miss you, Dad. Please come home soon." Your words struck the core of my soul. Suddenly, I saw it and I felt it—Amazing Grace, undeserved love. You were a little baby girl the last time I held you in my arms. "Mi Hermosa Bebe." That is what I used to call you. Today, you've grown. You've learned to walk, you've learned to talk, and you've learned to love without me.

I see your beautiful smile and your pretty face and I know it's always been true, God's Amazing Grace. I can finally see it. I never did anything to deserve you, Mi Hermosa Bebe. Your love is the force that drives me everyday to become a better man. Your words inspire me everyday to love and forgive, even when I'm hurting. When I see you, I see the undeserved love of God in your beautiful face. Mi Hermosa Bebe, you have brought happiness back into my life.

FATHER TO SON
Johnny S.

Prison life is harsh. Many lives were brought to a painful end, with both blood and tears being shed. Love had grown cold! This is where men became monsters and some became girls. I, too, grew indifferent as my world grew dark, blackened by the emptiness of life and lack of purpose.

Then one day, a small ray of light lit a small part of my heart, my son. In him, I sensed something that I had lost long ago—my innocence, the pureness of love. My little boy became a driving force in my life, a reason to love again. My little boy cheerfully and lovingly clung to me as I walked into the visiting room.

Our weekend visits usually began with hugs and kisses, escalating quickly to food and games. My little boy was always thrilled with spending time with his dad, especially when he won at every game. He understood very little about the harsh reality of prison life and fought hard to hold back the tears knowing that soon, he would have to say goodbye.

"I want to live with you dad" was my son's plea at the conclusion of visiting, his little hand holding my hand, as I leaned forward to kiss my wife goodbye. The gentle power of his words sliced through my heart. While filled with joy at my son's love and admiration, I was shocked that my nine year old would want to live in prison. The horror of one day sharing a cell with my son overwhelmed me with dread. Why would he want to live in a cage?

A sick, chilling sensation crept from between my shoulder blades and up the nape of my neck. Kneeling, I wrapped my arms around my son and hugged him protectively, as if my embrace could shield him from the world. "Never," I vowed to myself, "will he know the darkness within this world."

That day, something awoke within me that had long laid dormant—a realization that I must make the right choices in my life, to be the example that my son needs to help him build his own. I vow to become the father to my son that I never had.

FIRST TRUE LOVE
Bradley F.

I was running the streets when my pager went off. I was going to be late getting to the hospital, something I promised wouldn't happen. There was going to be hell to pay. It was after 4 o'clock in the morning when I finally arrived, two hours after ShawnTaé had been born, January 9, 1988—my first True Love.

There she was, sucking on her thumb as she lay sleeping, not yet one day old. Everything in my life had just changed. ShawnTaé was born 7 pounds 2 ounces, with a head full of hair and my heart in her hands.

CONTAGIOUS
Oscar R.

Stepping through the portal, I see my precious angel standing short and beautiful—illuminated by her crown of morning sun, star-sparkling eyes, and an upside-down rainbow painted on her lips by a heart flooding with colorful joy. She's an exact image of her mother—God's double-scoop of caramel-covered butter-pecan ice cream, my favorite!

The moment our eyes meet, Angeline runs to me, smiling brighter with each step. My little girl jumps into welcoming arms, warming my heart with her lovely voice, melting it like butter, with "I love you, Daddy."

She spreads the vibrant colors of her heart upon my cheeks with tender kisses, infecting me with joy. I kiss my princess on the cheek, lingering purposefully, provoking innocent giggles with my tickling mustache. When our laughter subsides, she looks back at my wife, then at me, and shouts excitedly, "Mommy says I can have her hug and kiss, too." I smile, surrendering to irresistible charm.

The gloom of that place beyond the portal disappears instantly, as I am unable to withstand my daughter's rainbow-bright smile.

OUR LAST VISIT
Victor G.

The last time I saw you was at the county jail. Your li'l hand was picking at the side of the glass window trying to remove the caulking. "Don't worry daddy, I'll get you out." Your mother choked the phone with her furious grip, crying at your inability to understand that it was not that easy for me to go home with you. That was seven years ago. Soon, it will be eight, nine, ten, and so on, until God says otherwise. I'll be here, never hearing from your mother or you. You might never remember that last visit, since you were but three, but I will always remember. Our last visit kills me slowly.

MORE THAN A CHRISTMAS GIFT
Oscar M.

The snow softly covered the ground. It hung elegantly on trees and bushes. The smell of freshly-cut pine clothed my mind. The anticipation was wonderful.

As a boy, I had always dreamed of getting toys, not my usual Christmas fare of clothes—socks mostly, pants, and an occasional jacket. But on this day, nearly 30 years ago, my stocking was filled with the biggest and brightest of gifts. That day, even the Grinch wore a smile. It was beyond special, a gift of all gifts. Expensive? You bet, beyond value. Precious? Indeed, a treasure! In God's eyes, I was deemed worthy. I fell deeply in love, head over heels—a timeless gift of inspiration. A surge of power. My soul smiles still.

December 20, 1983. Heaven's Macy's delivery: a cozy blue blanket, cocooning a baby boy! I held him in my arms. I felt like a giant. No, more like King Kong.

Today, he's a young man, though still my baby boy. More than a Christmas gift, a source of love. I love you, my Ito.

And Margaret, as a child, I grew up having many wishes, none so rewarding, however, as your love. Truly, I am blessed! I love the blooming roar of our grandchildren! Brightly, they shine with your smile.

Today, I wish for only one thing—to hold you in my arms. In the warmth of the day and the cold of the night, I close my eyes to hold my family tight!

PART 3. CRIME AND PUNISHMENT

Darkness cannot drive out darkness:
Only light can do that.
Hate cannot drive out hate:
Only love can do that.

- Martin Luther King, Jr.

HOKA HAY
Johnny S.

I staggered, bouncing off walls to the echo of voices piercing the hazy fog of unconcern. After the slow distilling of rotten apples sweating death, I smiled, blue flame astride brown horse, the ultimate chaser.

Slowly I drifted in and out of consciousness, oblivious to the commotion around me, as the vision of a painted Apache appeared in the mist of confusion atop a white-faced Appaloosa on a grassy ridge.

"Aho, brother," defiant, obsidian eyes ablaze in mischief. The unsmiling wrinkles of misery's past seasons record, as their long gray manes swirled as one in the gentle breeze.

Muffled screams intruded, "Why is my body dragged across cold cement slabs?"

I felt the galloping horse course through my veins, its deadly toxin tightens the reins of my pulse—beat, beat, beat. The beast, seeming to understand, slows its pace, allowing darkness to swallow my pain.

Hear me great spirit.
OyeheloTankashela.
I am cloud.
Hoka Hay.
It's a good day to die.

CONSUMED
Craig H.

My wants and desires were endless: greed consumed me. My thoughts concentrated not so much on dreams as results. My dreams had given way to shelter living; piles of donated clothes from the backs of trucks; stained tile floors; drab-colored metal bunk beds; and strands of hair in the Quaker's Oatmeal and grits.

I blamed my mother for my daily hunger and felt invisible to a world enslaved by the mighty dollar. My mind wandered enviously: no picket fence with fine grass, no security, no loving home. Dreams were about material gratification. I moved from one crime to the next, enriching my life with money that wasn't mine.

And I continue to want, beyond reason—money, love, comfort, remedies to the wounds unseen. Will I ever be free of my sinful desires? Was it worth the imprisonment of my gifted potential? Swallowed whole by the mouth of greed, here I remain.

PAPER PLANES
Patrick A.

The judge sat behind an imposing booth of polished wood. The black of his robe blended with the glossy leather of his gigantic chair, swallowing him up till he seemed little more than a floating head. Behind him, book-ended by two flags, loomed the Great Seal of California—a golden disk of rising sun.

"Mr. Foreman," the judge called solemnly, "May we please have your verdict?" The room froze in the distant hum of the cooling system.

Mr. Jury Foreman, standing in his box, folded the verdict into tiny paper planes and launched them from his lips, "We find the defendant guilty."

The polished walls of the courthouse lurched to one side and groaned as the first plane slammed into my mother's chest. An inhuman shriek escaped from the back of her throat, like that squelch of air that screeches from the stretched mouth of a child's balloon, a yelp so primordial that everyone, even the self-satisfied District Attorney, turned in amazement toward the woman who sat silently in the first row, who had suddenly remembered to breathe. No longer amused, they turned back to the golden seal and the foreman's tiny planes—except for me.

I swear, my mother hadn't taken a single breath since my trial began. At, "All rise," she either stopped breathing or forgot how or simply refused. Somehow, she found oxygen and strength enough in the salty pools ever brimming about her eyes. Her heart, cemented together by my gaze, began to shatter.

Another hijacked plane barreled in, this time slamming her soul. She broke. Tears leapt from her eyes to teeter upon the prayer-worn banister that separates freedom from condemnation, finding a home in my own.

As I stood behind the defense table, my knees shook till the ground disappeared under the weight of her distress. First one level, then the next, came crashing down, pan-caking to each boom of my heart.

Helpless, I offered my best, "It's okay, it's alright" smile—a weak salve to assuage her brokenness, piloted by the hand of my terrorism.

ENCOUNTER
Nick F.

Black bomber jacket and beanie pulled down to my eyes. Nike shoes laced up tight for the journey ahead. 2am, patrolling cold, dark back streets for rival soldiers. Buzzing sound from night dew resting on power lines. Dogs bark in the distance as approaching headlights catch my attention. My hand acts as a shield from the lights, checking for police sirens. My heart pounds like an Indian powwow drum. Butterflies fill my stomach as lights grow near.

Cold steel concealed beneath my jacket pressing against my stomach. A parked truck becomes a barrier to the approaching car. Engine grows louder and brakes squeak to a stop. My pistol, half way out, in anticipation of a gun battle. Time stops, as I wait for the next move.

An arm slowly appears. A voice erupts from the dark window, "Excuse me, can you direct me back to the freeway?" A moment of relief, as I provide directions to a woman and her kids. My focus returns to the tension-filled streets; I continue my patrol.

TRICKING FOR TREATS
Patrick A.

Where I grew up, young mothers still whisked their children across manicured lawns this time each year to knock on the doors of better neighborhoods—where kids could walk in safety, and king-sized Snicker bars filled plastic Jack O' Lanterns of every toothless "Twick-ohh-Tweet-er!"

The foggy night yawned, stretching its moist blackness across ghetto streets—dead except for the dealers, fiends and ho's. Creeping forward, I flashed my lights: off-on-brights-off and on again, signaling *"Don't Shoot."* I couldn't see them, but I knew they were there. The back of my neck could sense their warm fingers on cold steel, shooting me with their eyes.

Halloween in the hood puts everyone on edge. To a gangster, it's a night when confusion invites mayhem, and wickedness rules. It's killing time and every homeboy knows it.

Just in case, once more, I flashed my lights.

Back alleys and side streets open to boulevards lined with thumping mini-trucks and classic rides reflecting gas station lights.

Rounding the block, I saw her. Pushing herself from the curb, she stepped to my passenger-side window as I glided to a stop. Cheap perfume leaned in, bummed a cigarette, then a light. Thick mascara squinted against a wisp of smoke, and in the reddish-orange glow of tobacco, I watched valleys form in the corners of her eyes.

Customers called her "Cinnamon"; but, to me, she was just plain Cindy—from Mrs. Wolf's third-grade homeroom. We grew up running these streets: I slung dope and she, herself. The years were not kind to either of us. Not much had changed during the time I'd been away, except her makeup seemed a little more caked on.

Wrapping herself in child-like excitement, she righted herself to give me a practiced spin, a sultry showing of her wares. She wore a French maid's outfit, black with a frilly white apron over fishnets; *uber* skimpy and airbrush–tight. Crinkling her eyes, not from smoke this time, she asked, "Do you like my costume? Cute, right?"

In her smile still lived that little girl who reminded me of days before the dope game and her ho-stroll—of two kids Trick-o-

Treating and swapping my sour apple Jolly Ranchers for her watermelon sticks.

"Be safe, Cindy," I heard myself say, like so many times before. *"You, too"* kissed my cheek as the light turned green. In my rearview mirror, Cindy faded to Cinnamon, shaking her ass from one corner to the next.

Slinking back to the side streets that funnel into alleyways, I made my way to the next drop as Zeppelin's *Kashmir* vibrated the door panel that hid the package, and I found myself wondering, *"Why not? Why shouldn't a hooker have Halloween?"*

Turning the corner, off-on-brights-off-on... *"Don't Shoot."*

PRIDE AND PROMISES
Bernie F.

Springtime on the playground, laughing with ten-year old friends at a new school. A smack to the head, I turn to see Kevin charging at me. Is this a game? Confusion sets in as he lands punch after punch, screaming, "Defend yourself…fight back!" I try, but not knowing how to fight, I turn and walk away, hurt and crying inside. I try to forget about it.

Tomorrow will be better, I thought, but it only got worse. The bumps and bruises did not hurt as much as the abandonment by my friends. Being alone and ignored began eating me up. I swore that no one would challenge me again without a fight. I began to look for any challenge, even if it didn't concern me. If someone else was being taunted, I would jump in.

The fall term in junior high school created a different monster that graduated to the prestige of actual weapons—no longer satisfied with just fist fights. A bat, a screwdriver, a two-by-four, a knife, a hammer, even guns, were commonplace. I used them without thought as to their potential danger.

Sent to prison for murder as a teenager, I had no idea what to expect. Hearing one crazy, violent story after another scared me, something I dared not voice to anyone. I embraced the unwritten codes of prison conduct, like armor shielding my deeply hidden fears. The first rule: *Don't let anyone disrespect you.* Retaliation must be cold and swift, without thought, without warning.

Such thinking lasted more than twenty years, sending me to ten straight years in a security housing unit before its insanity snapped me back to reality. I set my mind to changing by making positive choices, understanding victim's awareness, going to church, and leaving behind any crowd that held those self-destructive beliefs.

That ugly part of me was gone and had no control over me, or so I thought. Come wintertime, I finally had a job to be proud of, working at a prison shop. I quickly climbed the responsibility ladder by learning to operate every work station. One day, an inmate was constantly making mistakes, making my job harder. I decided to check on his machine, again; maybe it just needed to be re-calibrated.

Before I could say a word, he went off. "What now? What do you want? What? What? What?" Instinctively, a bell went off in my head. 'He's yelling at me; he's disrespecting me!" No way! Unacceptable!"

As he continues running his jibs, I stare at his throat. I visualize plunging a screwdriver into his neck, over and over. STOP. I step back, trying to shake off the obsession. I notice that others are frozen, watching the scene. My mind spins again. "This has to be dealt with—now." I stay clam, telling him, "Don't trip." And I walk away.

But the compulsion of getting a weapon is still there, intensified by the imagined smell of blood spilled across his work station. I search for the tool man, but he is away from the shop. Furious, I sit and wait.

The break allows me to re-think what just happened. I am concerned at how quickly I had obsessed and wanted to act on this simple provocation. I wonder: what is more important to me—violently righting a supposed wrong, or keeping a promise I had made to my dying mother?

She had asked me to stop fighting and to be good. "I will," I promised her. That promise was the anchor that helped me maintain my sanity and diminish my rage. But a nagging disgust persisted: "What is wrong with you?"

FROM DEATH TO LIFE
David B.

The gun was in my face, and knew I was going to die. I was fourteen years old and had wanted a pair of Air Jordan Nikes real bad. I couldn't ask my grandma or great grandma to spend that kind of money, so I decided I was going to steal the shoes somehow. I stole the left shoe off the display shelf at one mall, and the right shoe at another.

I was so excited that I had finally got me some Jordans. I immediately put them on. On my way home I was approached by two guys I knew. One of them pulled a gun out and put it in my face and told me to come out of my shoes. My life flashed before me, and all I could think was that I was going to die for a pair of Air Jordans that I stole. I decided it was not worth it and went home in a pair of sandals I had in my backpack.

I paroled from prison three years later for a robbery I committed when I was sixteen. A week later, my "homies" and I were searching for prospective robbery victims, when we saw four guys. I pulled a gun and made them lie in the street. We took their jewelry, money...everything.

The irony! I was now the one with the gun, inflicting fear in other human beings. Surely, they were as scared as I was when I had my Air Jordans taken from me, but I didn't care. I created many victims as a gang member, something I am not proud of.

Years later, as I think about those I robbed, I wonder: did they think that was their last moment on Earth, that they might never see their families again? I had felt that fear, so I imagine those I victimized felt the same. I think back to a time when I called a guy from a rival gang over to my car. As I put the gun to his stomach, what were his thoughts as I carelessly pulled the trigger? I didn't like being shot at or staring down the barrel of a gun, but I was quick to shoot or pull a gun on someone else. Such hypocrisy! I am truly ashamed of myself, and I pray for the forgiveness of those I have victimized.

MOMENTUM
Joe A.

The officer arrives to discover twenty-seven-year-old Carlos dead from a gunshot wound. Across town, a kid wakes up screaming. He's frightened, but doesn't know why. He cries out for his father, but his calls go unanswered. Crawling out of bed, he peeks through the half-cracked door of his parents' bedroom—telephone thrown on the floor, his mother on the bed, knees clutched to her chest, slowly shaking her head. "No! No! No!"

What this boy—and so many like him—do not yet understand is that, at such moments, their lives will change dramatically. Their hopes and dreams were shattered the moment the bullet left the barrel, their futures evaporating, like that trail of smoke, into the night. As each bullet spirals toward its target, every rotation claims another victim, annihilating the hopes and dreams of countless more.

Gone are the hopes of a little boy who, holding his father's hand, walks to his first day of school: he is left to walk alone. Of a young man yearning for the embrace of his father, to ease the pain of his first broken heart: his father is not there. Of a little sister, needing her big brother's protection from the bully next door: she must fend for herself. Of a little girl kneeling at her bedside every night, praying with all her heart that her brother comes home: her prayers go unanswered. Of the young lady who dreams of dancing with her brother at her Quinceanera: the music plays, but she dances alone. Of a mother dreaming that her son will recover from his addictions, return home, hold her in his arms, and say "Mom, I love you": but her broken heart knows that day will never come.

After twenty-five years, the bullet has not lost its momentum. No one can stop it.

LIFE OF THE LIVING DEAD
Brian L.

Zombies, that's what we are. We few, we most miserable few. Life for a life: and it's a civilized death sentence for me. We live, but we are the dead, foolishly enduring while knowing life is over, yet still animated—life without parole.

Each night, I return to my tomb, an eight-by-twelve world, consumed with what lies beyond this Necropolis of ghosts. Some days a semblance of life begins: a job to do, a phone call to make, a letter to write. With the march of time, the bright days are far too few.

We zombies consume and take, but never produce or contribute. Cut off from the living, we seek any signs of real life. We hope to return from the grave, to resurrect from the dead.

Are we truthfully unredeemable? Has the kinder, gentler killing that is life without parole really served justice? If I had been an animal, there would be groups protesting this inhumane caging. The night comes, and the zombie returns to his tomb; the world shrinks back to eight-by-twelve.

As the decades roll by, like months to a normal life, I continue trudging toward an unknown goal, obscured by time—for the sake of justice. It would have been more merciful to end it, ages ago.

THE LOADED GUN
Gerardo L.

The gun is partially loaded, motionless on the coffee table. I'm sitting on a couch right in front of it, almost as still as the gun. My mind wanders as I stare at its deadly cargo. When last did I shoot it? Two hours ago? Three? Four or five? Does it matter? Nothing, nobody, is going to stop me from using it again.

I pick it up with my right hand. "How can something so small be so lethal?" I try to remember the lives it has taken. Five? Six? Was it seven? Those are just the ones I knew. There are others, thousands, I never knew. No matter.

I'm going to keep playing this game: I don't care what my chances are. Russian Roulette—Mexican style.

My heart races. I press the gun gently against my skin. Bam! It breaks my skin and rips into a vein. Not a .38 or a .357, but 80 cc's of a dark brown, deadly relief explode into my bloodstream. Anger, resentment, disappointment, and bitterness evaporate. Enjoy the ride for as long as it lasts. I know it's so wrong; but it feels so good. Nothing matters. I close my eyes and drift away.

Two hours later, I open my eyes—back to reality, back to my misery. I hate my parents, I hate society, I hate myself. Yet death has spared me once again.

LIFE WITHOUT
Patrick A.

S oft as snow, a purity of light descends from above. Immersed in serenity beyond description, golden rays illuminate my soul. All around is darkness, yet I am engulfed in grace as I ascend, secure in my faith…of another day in prison.

Each morning, I kneel upon an icy concrete floor, at an alter of a tombstone. I beat my chest humbly, and beg forgiveness. I seek neither heavenly riches, nor the salvation that maketh all things anew. Oh, that Providence might have mercy upon me—sinner, heretic, pagan, and ever-pious agnostic. I prefer esoteric, if I must be labeled.

Although branded by atheism, I fervently hope for the Hereafter, even as I profess faith only in the Here and Now. Be it reincarnation or Glory Land, I ponder such lofty matters because I have sure fouled up this life.

My lot has been cast, condemned to Life without Parole (LWOP), the State's way of saying "die in a cage like an old dog." A friendly execution that no one decries as being either too cruel or sufficiently unusual. There will be no fanfare, media blitz, state-appointed appellate attorneys, or candle-lit vigils to count down the eleventh hour. The Death Penalty with a smile.

I realize I will die behind these walls, and I can do nothing to alter my fate. I have made peace with this fact, as I strive to be the best I can be. A contrite heart, not religiosity, drives my recovery. Every good deed is in honor of lives torn asunder. Each day is lived in amends to all whom I have harmed.

I have walked down the dismal wasteland of insanity and returned to reclaim my humanity. From tutoring inmates for the G.E.D., to charity drives, to counseling at-risk youth, to earning an Associates degree, I am an example to my peers that genuine change is possible.

By helping even one inmate to turn from crime, I will prevent senseless victimization. When I die, I will just be dead. But before I die, I will have made the world a safer place. Life without parole does not have to mean life without hope.

COUNTING TIME
Bernie F.

870,048,000 seconds. I hated rock music, especially AC/DC and heavy metal; it infuriated me. I grew to resent former friends and imaginary enemies: human life lost its value.

14,500,800 minutes. Placed in a cage to contain the animal fury. Wicked habits and the inmate code ruled. Don't associate with anyone outside your race. Don't share, accept, drink after, or eat with anyone outside the group.

241,680 hours. False pride, conceit, and evil overrun me. Hope has left the building. Cynical laughter echoes in a dark and hollow brain.

10,707 days. Death seems the only escape from a concrete coffin, never to return, or ever see, the outside world. A stabbing, a fight, a slicing, another stabbing, another slicing, and another fight—each mindless act calculated to end the nightmare by way of the gunner's nine-millimeter.

14,333 weeks. The thunderous storms begin to subside. A little light shines and overpowers the injustices. There must be a better way. How dumb to have fallen into such a lifestyle! Really tired, the weight is unbearable, need to change. The bottom is truly lonely.

331 months. I begin to love rock—classic, heavy, or soft. But I still can't figure the metal head-bangers. I overcome resentments, seeing others for their goodness. These are huge accomplishments. Blessings abound.

27 ½ years, give or take a few seconds, minutes, hours, or days. This lifer, serving a first-degree murder sentence, is found suitable for release, no longer a risk to society. With a snap, God's mercy and compassion have lifted the greatest burden from my shoulders.

To whom much is entrusted, much is expected. My responsibility is clear. Stay tuned, my proudest moment is yet to come.

CRYSTAL DEATH
Johnny S.

My heart beat with Ralfi Pagan's "To Say I Love You" in a smoked-filled room, as tiny crystals dissolved, like melting snow, in a stainless steel spoon. A chemical odor turned my stomach into a sea of fluttering butterflies. My six-shooter cocked and loaded with 30 cc's of poison. "Pop pop." The tip finds the super highway to hell. I fired the shot, polluting all that was good. My head imploded with a fiery madness of pleasure. Tears stained my face, a trail of mistakes temporarily forgotten. My new love was evident in my desire for more, to forget life's pain.

And now, I can't help wondering, if I hadn't fired the shot, would I be here today?

THIS DAMNED MIRROR SHOWS NO MERCY!
Brian L.

Seeing the brutal truth in my reflection makes me cringe. The 23-year-old scar tracing my jaw line recalls a childish BB-gun fight. A mole on my nose, appearing shortly after my birth, conjures each taunt or cruel remark from schoolboys otherwise forgotten. The divot above my left eye marks the impact of the raging right hook of a drunken step-father. The pock marks above my cheek denote a teenage bout with chicken pox. The freckles that dot my face still whisper my mother's comforting words, "They're called 'angel kisses,' baby."

Each scar, blemish, and wrinkle helps to tell my soul-crushing story. But the worst, the most painful vision, is those eyes staring coldly back at me, eyes that beheld the foulest torments and cruelties, sometimes by others, mostly by me—fearful orbs that ridicule and condemn. I struggle to confront that image with a willingness to forgive.

AN INNOCENT MAN
Richard G.

My cell door opens with a squeak. I make a mental note to remind maintenance to oil it again. I pass through the doorway with a slightly disgusted look and a shake of the head. No sooner had I exited my cell than it was forgotten, pushed to the box marked "things to do," in the back of my mind.

Awareness kicks in as I make my way to chow, marching down the tier, head straight, eyes everywhere I need them to be. Giving my neighbor a nod, I push on. By the time I get to the stairwell, he's forgotten, too. I've passed his door countless times, not once having the desire to turn my head towards his door. Everything I need to know about him, I know: he's not my race, and he's not from my gang—end of story. Never once had I turned my head towards him nor looked into his cell.

One day I awoke to the sound of rain pattering endlessly upon my narrow window. The smell of wet concrete filled my cell, as the ache in my bones told me, "Today is going to be a cold one." I looked out my window and watched the clouds cry as I drank my morning coffee. The familiar squeak of my door yelled "Chow time," and once again, I put on my game face. Just before exiting, I reached for my waistband and gave my shank a playful tap. "Wait!" my senses screamed. Something is different. I measured my surroundings and noticed my neighbor was not at his door.

For the first time, I became curious about him. As I passed his door, it took all I had to keep my head straight, but my prison eyes caught a figure squatting on the floor. "What the fuck," I thought to myself as I broke my step. Gathering myself, I pushed.

On my way back, after chow, I couldn't help myself. I peered into his cell, shocked at what I saw. He was painting on a homemade easel propped up on his toilet seat, while he sat atop a makeshift stool of rolled-up blankets. My eyes took in everything, but they were rooted on the painting.

It was of a college campus—Stanford, to be exact; and it was beautiful. I was shocked. I thought only Mexicans could draw. I felt his eyes on me: I was caught. He smiled at me and asked if I liked it.

"Yes," I stammered, somewhat embarrassed. I couldn't help myself: I wanted to talk to this man. I wanted to know how he could paint with such elegance, but I didn't know the words. He saw my hesitation, and smiled once more, knowingly. He began to ask me questions. We were suddenly having the first of many conversations. He told me he was a trained painter and that the painting was for his mom, a professor at Stanford University. Again, I was shocked.

As time went on, I guess you could say we became friends, or as close to it as two in our situation could be. The only thing I had a problem with was that he always told me he was innocent—falsely accused of murder. I'd tell him to take that shit to the chaplain 'cause we're all guilty.

Ten years passed. I'd been transferred all over the state. One day, I was watching a documentary on PBS about people falsely accused—and the assistance California gave to them upon their release. Once again, I was shocked by my former neighbor, his face smiling at me from a 13-inch TV, as it hit me: I had met an innocent man.

THE NIGHT CHRISTMAS DIED
Patrick A.

On the longest night of their lives, a young wife and child helplessly watched as his life poured out onto a cold cement floor. A husband, father, and provider lay bleeding. Encircling him like a babe in a manger, they had yet to realize Christmas is lost. Their only concern: "Where is the damned ambulance?"

Behold, a neon sign appears in the East (of Los Angeles). Locals heard the call of the blast and came to witness. Wise men, led by a 911 call, arrived in a wagon of chrome and flashing lights. They came bearing gauze, defibrillators, and morphine. Too late—a life had been extinguished.

There is something visceral, palpable about the Holiday season. Carols take over the airways, holiday specials dominate television, and parades invade Main Street. Dads untangle Christmas lights in the front yard, and children grow giddy with anticipation. Seasonal mementos are taken from the attic and hung with care. Pine trees scent homes and mistletoe dangles invitingly overhead. It is the most wonderful time of the year. Messages of "Peace on Earth" and "Be of good cheer" bombard the psyche.

But...what of those who do not share in the season's delight? The more others rejoice, the more miserable I become. Every image of a wholesome family smiling around the dinner table, piled high with roast turkey and honey-baked ham, weighs me with shame and remorse, like the chains of Jacob Marley.

Sleigh bells were jing–jing–jingling, when a shotgun blast pierced the air. Red and blue strobes from a black-and-white cast a surreal pallor across candle–filled windowpanes. Bright yellow Caution tape, like streamers of strung popcorn, adorned the perimeter of the crime scene.

The spirit of Holiday cheer splattered the wall and cash register. A family mourns a lethal silent night. For them—and for me—there will be no more festivities or Yuletide glee. Every catchy jingle and heartfelt happy holiday greeting rips open the wounds. Every nicety is a sad reminder of the tragic night when Christmas died—when a man was brutally murdered.

ME
Kevin H.

Granite walls formed and fashioned from the sweat of the brow ages upon ages ago, prehistoric gun towers and chiseled signs welcomed you to Folsom State Prison.

At nineteen, I thought I had a world of experience and everything figured out. Yet, violence, hate, anger, and malice soon became realities through the screams that penetrated the cold steel bars. Fear bellowing from within, I tried hard to choke them back, to keep them deeply buried within. I recalled, from some movie, a lingering scene of red lipstick scrawled across a mirror, "The anticipation of death is worse than death itself."

School was in session and I was the pupil, entering through the gates into a world of the unexpected, clueless as to who I would become.

Drawn into a new dimension, I was given new identities of "homeboy," "youngster," "white boy," and "brother," from those I scarcely knew. Boot camp was at hand, "prison style." A new life began to take shape, and survival was the key.

Years later, I graduated with honors, diploma written in bold black, "Validated Prison Gang Member." Like a ravenous pit bull, I strived to reach the top of my new False Identity. Fifteen years of resting with the Pelicans, surrounded by California Redwoods, and trapped within a concrete steel box, I had reached the end.

Engulfed inside the gates of propaganda and prison politics, my life ran aimlessly. Hope was lost, my future knocking at Death's gate. Who was I? Who had I become? I was lost behind a dark mask of False Identity.

As I lay wasting away in my concrete cubicle, a voice belched out, "Last two!" I responded with, "four-nine." A smile began to form across my face, as I recognized the name in the left-hand corner of the envelope—a girl whom I hadn't seen nor heard from in over twenty years. Glorious childhood memories of Black Cat firecrackers and pop bottle rockets flashed through my mind.

Heather was her name—a distant cousin I'd lost through my life of insanity. She reminded me of what I had abandoned so long ago— the everlasting love of family.

Lost in delusion, yet refusing to let go of my proclaimed identity, I received more and more letters sharing her love and, more importantly, that of God. Emblazoned upon the envelopes were scriptures from the Bible. Fueled by the power of the penetrating words I didn't want to hear, her hundred-and-five pounds of country-girl doggedness persisted, until those Holy Scriptures began to penetrate the marrow of my hardened soul.

Heather was determined to pull away the mask of deception I had worn for so long. In 2004, her diligent work drew me to my knees, as I surrendered my life to Jesus. Through His patience, mercy, and grace, I'm being molded anew, with a new identity. Jesus Christ introduced me to someone in prison: his name is Kevin.

SHIPWRECKED
Ralph P.

As I tried to navigate my way through the choppy seas and narrow straights of my existence, I was concerned only with docking in paradise—easy money, beautiful women, and a kick-back lifestyle.

At the bow of my ship, I could see the lovely, wealthy, and luxurious. I could almost grasp the pleasures. But with my vessel, nobody was at the helm. And when I took the wheel, I would always seem to take on water, steer off course, or break down entirely, setting myself adrift in perilous seas.

As I sailed recklessly through life, I was offered help several times. But my pride and ego wouldn't allow it; I always declined help. Resorting to pillage and plunder, I pirated my way from crisis to crisis. Finally, wanted and on the run, I commandeered an abandoned vessel and immediately ran aground. And now, in the most desperate conditions imaginable, I am hopelessly defeated—shipwrecked, for decades.

63 DAYS
Charles H.

What if I had carried out the plans my parents had for me? I graduated Santa Monica High and enrolled in UCLA. With a BA in business, I would have had the choice of running my father's body and fender shop or my grandfather's mortuary. But after 63 days, my life took a tragically different course. I had dropped out of college and got swept up in a life of crime. What if I had obtained my BA in Business? My father wouldn't have lost the body and fender shop, and I wouldn't have hurt so many people. I could have enjoyed a good life with my family and friends. I could have created a family of my own.

"What if?" is torturous for me, because I had been blessed with opportunities, had I only taken advantage of them. Damn. If I'm given a chance at release, I'll know what to do and I will be successful. Failure is not an option.

SO THEY SAY
Colin S.

So they say that criminality is a choice, that people in prison have chosen a life of crime, and they are solely responsible for their actions. In a general sense, they are. If we look at the "facts" of the matter, they have made a choice. No one was holding a gun to their head and, thus, they are responsible for their actions. But truth and facts don't always equate.

If we look at the "truth" of the matter, most people in prison grew up disenfranchised, in marginalized communities where criminality is often a part of the culture, while mainstream society poses as the enemy—either actively attacking them or passively excluding them. From this perspective, crime looks less like a conscious, informed choice, and more like a product of limited choices, and a lack of education and positive role models.

This isn't to say that someone in prison is somehow less responsible for their actions. This does not negate personal responsibility or mitigate what they have done. But it poses an interesting question: "What part do I play in my community where my neighbor guns down 30 people in a movie theater?"

PART 5. LOSS

Ever has it been that love knows not its own depth until the hour of separation.

- Kahlil Gibran

SHE SPOKE
Bernie F.

It wasn't until the age of 38 that I finally felt the sadness of death. My mother had a brain aneurism and went into shock while visiting family in Mexico. The doctor found a pear-sized tumor in her right temple and removed it. Tests and exams showed the tumor to be malignant, and the cancer was spreading. No treatment would change the outcome. She was given only months to live.

I was faced with losing a loved one for the first time. As I sat in prison for my twenty-second year, the thought had crossed my mind several times before about how I would deal with such a tragedy. What would I feel? How would I react? Would I act out? I definitely would not share my feelings. No, those would stay inside. I would call home and talk to her on speaker so she could hear my voice.

After the calls she would ask my sister, "When can I see my boy?" After a couple of months she could barely eat and stopped talking all together. Two of my nieces brought her to prison for our final visitation July 23, 2006.

What happened at our last visit changed me forever. I gave her a hug and many kisses, as she beamed with joy. My nieces said that she had been so excited since the day before, when they had told her she would visit her son. I remember telling her how much I loved her, and that she was the best Mom I could ask for. Then, something inside pushed me to say, "Mom, forgive me for not being a better son." She spun her head to the right, not wanting me to see her face, and said, "No, you forgive me for not being a better mother." Both nieces looked at each other, exclaiming, "She spoke."

But what I had seen in her eyes before she turned was the deep pain, guilt, and hurt of a mother who carried the blame for the terrible crimes her son had committed, a son who had joined a gang, dropped out of school, and run away from home; who had become a murderer, been in prison since the age of 16, stabbed several prisoners, and spent 12 years in solitary confinement with no contact visits.

The weight of all this, she endured as her responsibility. How immature and selfish of me for not seeing this before. She turned to me and insisted, "You have to stop fighting and be good."

"I will Mom," I promised. How could I deny her anything? One of the last things she said to me was, "You will get out soon, Mijo. Just be good." It was the shortest visit ever, but the most profound. I would never again cause the pain I saw in her eyes or inflict it upon anyone else.

BROKEN DREAMS
Bradley F.

It was Saturday morning and I couldn't wait. I was going to spend time with my Dad! Straight to the Ontario Airport, we grabbed a flight to San Francisco. I was so excited that I could barely sit still to be buckled into my seat. This was better than Disneyland, because I was getting my first ride in an airplane with my dad.

When we landed, my aunt greeted us with big hugs and kisses. "How's my favorite nephew?" (Really, I was her only nephew). Her next comment hurt. "Oh, you look so skinny! Doesn't your mother feed you?" I looked at my dad who was shaking his head. I was sure he was hoping that I would remain respectful.

We went sightseeing and after, we ate my favorite seafood—shrimp. Before the night ended, my dad tucked me in and told me to get a good night's sleep. He had a big day planned. I thought nothing could be as big as today.

The next morning, my dad woke me up early, pushed me into the bathroom to get cleaned up, and ordered breakfast. We took off to some sporting goods store where everything he bought me was silver and black. We were going to my first football game! The Raiders beat the Chiefs, of course, and I had the time of my life. After we flew home that night, my dad dropped me off. I fell into bed, wishing only to grow up and be like my dad.

That was the last time I would spend any meaningful time with him. Not because he passed away or did something to get locked up. It was simpler than that: he just stopped coming around.

After years of abandonment, my only question for him is, "Where did you go?" I vowed never to be like him. My two beautiful daughters have never had to wonder if I love them.

PAPA
Joe A.

I walked into the counselor's office. She told me to have a seat, that I had a phone call. I froze, knowing the terrifying reality that awaited me at the other end of that receiver. I was not ready to let go.

Last week Maria, my little sister, warned me to prepare myself. I found that statement so odd. How does one prepare for something like this? Since hearing the news that my father was terminal, I'd been feeling as if there is a barrier between the world and me.

Now here I was, confronted by life's eternal mystery—Death. I stood there, gripped by fear, overwhelmed by the moment, mesmerized by the receiver in the counselor's hand. It stared up at me like a viper about to inject its deadly venom into my body. I wanted to run from that office. If I don't hear the words, then it's not happening.

The counselor finally woke me from my stupor. With a trembling hand I reached for the phone and put it to my ear. I cringed, knowing that the crushing blow I was about to receive would penetrate the core of my soul. After a few seconds my mother's voice broke the silence. "He's gone. He left us, Mijo." My father was dead.

On April 16, 2010, death had reached out to tap me on the shoulder, reminding me of my arrogance and selfish pride. My soul was being vacuumed from my body, falling headlong into a vortex of whirling thoughts and emotions.

I wanted desperately to reach out and hug my mother. Her words were drenched in pain. I ached to hold and comfort her, thereby, perhaps, finding some comfort of my own. I dizzily grasped for support and guidance in the lonely chasm of pain and confusion, but found none.

How could my father have surrendered to death's silent whisper--this six-foot giant of a man, my father, whom I considered a God amongst mortals. The heroic tales my mother told of him are forever inscribed on my mind, a brave horseman from the golden hills of Hermosillo, a gentle soul whom I loved and respected.

Papa, as you look down on me from above I beg you, do so with favor. I am deeply sorry for the pain I caused you. Know that each day I strive to make you proud. I will carry your name with honor and with the same quiet dignity that characterized your life.

There are so many things I needed to tell you, but can't, because on this day God took your super powers away and made you mortal.

May the golden hues of heaven remind you of home.

THE WALK
Peter M.

998 was the year I took the walk to the programming office. It's the walk all prisoners dread. Now, for the first time in my incarceration, I was on my way there.

From the moment my cell door opened, I felt uneasy. My name over the P.A. system only confirmed that bad feeling. It seemed like they wanted you to take that walk. Nobody said anything. My mind was everywhere, because I'd heard no news of family being sick or hurt. I tried to set my mind at ease with thoughts like, "This doesn't have to be what it seems. I could be going for some other reason other than death."

As I neared the program office, reality tightened its chilling grip. I entered. Across from me was a sergeant. He told me to sit down and said that my sister, Theresa, had called and needed to talk to me. He handed me the phone. My sister said, "It's Angie. Peter, she's gone." My mind flooded with memories of our life. Theresa was still talking, but I couldn't hear. I thought of Angie and when we were children, maybe to keep the pain from taking over. I thought of all the good times, blocking out the reality of her death.

In a worldly sense, death is the owner of life, waiting patiently for the inevitability of its prize. I had surrounded myself with death. It became my constant companion. I reached a point where I considered myself immortal and death, my friend. I introduced it to others, imagining somehow that as long as I kept it fed, I could escape its grip.

Death visited me often. Those around me succumbed to its touch; yet I was spared. Was it a reprieve from some sort of pain, or was it to torture me with the anguish of seeing loved ones fade into the abyss? Every time someone around me died, a small part of my soul also died until, eventually, I was as dead as those I had buried. My passing, however, was all the more excruciating, because I lived.

THE OLD, THE SICK, THE DYING
Johnny S.

I was not interested in walking to chow. In fact, after 31 years in prison, somehow I had lost my appetite for dried-up, over-cooked fish that looked and tasted like cardboard. From the window of my cell door, I watched the flow of inmates moving in unison down a flight of stairs; cattle being led to pasture. Something caught my attention. At the bottom of the stairs sat an old man in a wheelchair. Prison had become a convalescent home and a graveyard of broken lives.

His name was George. He was a frail old man who looked out of place on a prison yard. His source of life was a breathing machine attached to the back of his wheelchair. As I continued to watch the old man, he appeared very confused, almost scared, as the steady flow of inmates moved past him, talking and laughing. I noticed that a few of the inmates intentionally looked away.

I was disappointed that not a single individual offered to help the old timer. When I asked my neighbor, "Why did you look away when you saw that old man?" He said, "I'm serving a life sentence. I don't want to see what I'm going to become." My disappointment gave way to anger, as I felt the "old" me resurface, and for a second, I welcomed an old familiar friend.

How could anyone be so heartless, to walk past a helpless old man without offering to help? Then it struck me! I know! It was me! I was one of those heartless people who would ignore those around me.

In that world, there was no kindness. Acts of compassion were a form of weakness. Greed was the motivation. I imagined I was indestructible and would live forever. My false sense of security led to a total disregard for human life. So how do I reclaim the kindness that was once part of my life?

In December 2010, old man George finally passed on, still wearing his prison blues. He went to rest with some of the best this prison has ever known. Now that he is gone, the legend lives on, of the frail old man in his chair.

We shared the dinner table on that first day I saw him, and I still remember what he told me: "There are no guarantees in life but one—death. It sucks being old. People walk by you like you don't exist." The lesson he passed on gave me a new perspective on life: treat others as you would want to be treated, and to cherish every day as if it were your last.

ANOTHER FUNERAL
Tyrone H.

There I stood, brother beside me, his comforting hand on my shoulder. I thought, "It's cold in here." My knees trembled, as I looked around the crowded church. I still couldn't see her. Edging closer and hiking myself up on my tippy toes, I grabbed the edge of the shiny, pink coffin and peeked inside.

The unmistakable scar across the bridge of her nose was all I saw—a scar she'd permit only me to trace with my fingers while I sat on her lap so many times before. My eyes flooded with tears as chills danced across my body. Still holding onto the edge of the coffin, trying to see inside, I was suddenly lifted off my feet by a strong arm.

I saw her now. She lay there—too peaceful to be real. Licking salty tears from the corners of my mouth, I watched her. In a voice I didn't recognize as my own, I whispered, "Wake up! Wake up!" She just lay there. I reached down and shook her shoulder, the way I'd done at home after I thought she'd had enough nap time. No response. I recall my lungs straining to get air as my young body was wracked by tears and grief. She didn't wake up. She never woke again.

...As the hot gun-powder breath of death erupted around our heads, we dove to the ground—not quickly enough. I lifted my friend and held him, facing me. Hot, sticky blood gushed from the hole in his head and covered my face, the copper-like taste assaulting my tongue. With each diminishing beat of his heart, more blood escaped from the perfect hole. He died in my arms in the back of a not-so-speeding truck, my finger in his head, as I tried to stop the blood that eventually stopped on its own.

I find myself alone, again, in the small, cold church. I sense death all around me, feel its hot dampness, smell its putrid dankness. Older now, I am still paralyzed by that familiar terror that keeps me from the coffin. I know it'll be her in the casket once again, as it had been that day long ago. Eyes shut tightly to blind me to the fear, I move closer and closer, unable to resist Death's pull. I peek in.

But it's not her this time: it's the old me—battered and bruised. I say my good-byes. I'm smiling, relieved to see him gone!

SAYING GOODBYE
Bradley F.

When I hung up the phone that night, I was confused and worried. She made me say goodbye. That was something we didn't do. I had a rough night, tossing and turning until my alarm went off.

I dragged myself out of bed for physical training, feeling that something wasn't right. Halfway through the day, I found out what that was. I was told to report to the Company Commander's Office. As I stepped into her office, I did a quick survey. My platoon sergeant and the First Sergeant were also there. "Reporting as ordered, ma'am." I was told to have a seat. This was all bad.

Captain Smith was strictly business. She went right to what she had to say. "At 0900 hours, I received a phone call informing me that your grandmother passed away last night." Those words hit me like the butt of my M-16 assault rifle—but with a pain I had never known. Then I heard, "Breathe, take a deep breath."

I was given 10 days emergency leave to be with my family. I was going to bury the love of my life. I had thought she would always be there for me. I had to say goodbye to my granny.

WITCH
Kevin H.

Clutching her hand, I looked into Grandma's eyes asking a simple childhood question, "When is your birthday?" With a quizzical answer she replied, "I'm a witch." My boyish glance, lost in space, tried to discern what that meant—a question I asked many times through the years, trying to discover Grandma's elusive answer about being a witch. A frightening chill left my spine tingling. Was Grandma possibly the wicked witch of Oz?

Grandma had a way of always appealing to her grandchildren's senses: home-cooked meals, stories of times past, fishing adventures across the Texas plains. Her Creek Indian features would sooth the soul of a wild beast. She was a mighty woman within a small frame.

No one ever saw the murderous attack coming, an attack set to steal, kill, and destroy. The haunted house of cancerous cells spread throughout her body, destroying every living organ in its wake. Potions brewed in the cauldrons of laboratories, radiation treatments, and morphine drips. Her fight for life continued. Beating away the flying monkeys set to destroy her, she grimaced at the routine hospice visits.

Ethel loved her family, always placing her children and grandchildren above herself. As Christmas approached, she was determined to hang on to the very end. On December 26, her last whisper, "Where's Kevin?" punctuates my enduring memory of this precious woman, though it took me a long time to understand Grandmas' quizzical tease about being a witch. Halloween was her birthday. Trick or Treat, Grandma!

MY ROCK
Richard G.

Honor is what pushed me, pride is what kept me, but love gave me the strength to change. I was taught to believe the lie that if you dropped out of the game, you were less than nothing.

I spied yet another man locking it up, no longer able to hang with the big boys. His head hung low on slumped shoulders as he passed my cell. I could smell defeat emitting from every pore; even his steps echoed weakness. "What a waste," I said, disgusted, as I turned from my cell window.

The world I lived in was hard, but we were taught that only as a group, as homies, could we strive. Anyone who decided to leave the fold, to drop out, was called a rat, a punk, no good, a bitch. They were nothing because they decided to do something else. It never occurred to me that maybe they just didn't want to hurt people anymore, or have to play the gangster all day.

All I knew was that I could never be nothing. I was Creeper, and I earned my stripes. My word was solid, and I had respect.

Then one day I got a visit from mom and my two sisters, my heart leaping for joy as they entered the visiting room. As they approached where I sat behind an inch of glass, I couldn't believe how beautiful my mom looked, her curly hair framing tired eyes. Just then, I noticed she had a cane. "What's wrong?" I asked. "Nothing Mijo, I just got back problems."

Who would have known that a killer was growing inside her and in a few short weeks, she would be bedridden in a hospital, fighting for her life? She fought for nine months before God saw it was time to call her home. I lost the greatest part of my life that day. I lost my mama, my rock.

That was the day change entered my life. Like a mustard seed, it grew, until years later, I was that man who passed my cell with his eyes to the ground. The days that led to my decision to drop are not important; what *is* important was my love for my family, my real family, and what they wanted for me.

I was a dropout, but I was a somebody.

"F" IS FOR "FANTASTIC"
Johnny S.

The alarm sounds. "GET DOWN!" Green pigs bark, chambering 0.223 caliber rounds into their HK Mini-14 rifles. In the center of the yard, an inmate bleeds, in dire need of medical attention.

Built at the end of the world to hide society's failure, Pelican Bay State Prison and its security housing unit serve as California's catacomb of misery designed to torture souls fallen from grace in a graveyard of rusting dreams.

Empty corridors echo with the clank of my leg irons and the dull thump of muddy prison boots. Tossed into a morgue of a cell, eeriness running across my flesh, I settle into a cold night under the shadow of darkness, and I reflect on my grandmother. A strong woman who didn't speak or understand English, she was loving and fearless, with no equal, a security blanket of comfort and safety, the thread that kept my sanity intact.

I remember seeing my name on the list of eighth-grade graduates. My grandmother was so proud of me. My truth to her: "F" stands for "fantastic." The fact that the school was simply looking to get rid of a bad apple without an education didn't matter; I was going to Disneyland, and Grandma was happy!

Two days passed since word of her death. A picture of her last day, etched in my heart, brought tears to my eyes and shook me to my core. Society and God had conspired to take away all that was good; I was filled with rage.

But who was I angry at? For years I'd lived a selfish life, thinking only of myself, never once believing I needed to say, "I love you," or "Thank you for being the loving grandmother you always were."

My heart drowns in shame and sorrow as I remember your last thoughts, scribed on a sign you held on your death bed, "Johnny, I love you."

Now, in the SHU, my mind often drifts
To a beautiful woman I sadly miss
From the sound of her voice and beauty in her eyes
Her courage, strength and determination
So full of life, yet, so patient
She stood by my side when no one else would
And brightened the days that no one else could
She gave me strength when I needed to be strong
And the wisdom to know right from wrong
Then I was struck with sudden departure
And oh how my days seemed so much darker
Now that she is gone and I'm all alone
Facing the struggles of life on my own
Now the sun doesn't seem so bright
And the clouds are grey when they used to be white
I've lost the will and strength to go on
Nothing to look forward to, now that she's gone
But then I remembered what she'd say to me
To always stay strong however hard it may be
To look inside myself whenever I felt scared
And find that inner strength she always said was there
I smiled cause she was right, and even though she's gone
I know if she were here, she'd want me to be strong
So I'll keep my hopes alive and hold my head up high
And when I'm feeling down, I'll look to the sky
Cause I know that you are watching, even as I speak
I love you grandma and may you now rest in peace...

PART 6. STRUGGLES

History, despite its wrenching pain, cannot be unlived, however, if faced with courage, need not be lived again.

- Maya Angelou

MONSTER OF PAIN
Robert G.

Silently, the faceless monster steps into the alleys of darkness, searching out his next victim—maybe a drunk coming out the back door of a bar, or a dope dealer looking for a customer—any easy target to rob for a quick few bucks will do. The Smith and Wesson Python tucked into the waistband of his black 560's provides his authority to overpower his prey.

Wreaking havoc upon his victims, inflicting pain, and humiliating them with fear, he slaps, punches, kicks and pistol whips. He terrorizes as he steals wallets, money, watches, jewelry, anything of value that can be traded or sold, never thinking that his cowardly acts will affect them for the rest of their lives. He not only creates painful memories, he robs them of any sense of security and well-being.

After years of staring into the small, six-by-four inch mirror provided in the state cell, and seeing the horrid reflection of the faceless monster he was, shame and guilt ate at him mercilessly.

He began searching to find himself, peeling the layers to discover that it was his own hurt that masked his true identity. As he slowly healed his pain, a face came into focus, revealing that the faceless monster is my former self.

AWAKENING
Johnny S.

The last sweet relic of my dream world begins to seep away. Stretching stiff muscles and aching bones going "snap, crackle and pop," I rise from bed to face the enraged beast within.

His onslaught begins abruptly with smashing blows of anger. Hate rings loudly in my ears. Merciless intent, crippling accusations of despair and failure. Soul crushing bouts of doubt and remorse continuously pummel my tortured soul. Unfortunately, my day has just begun.

Staggering forward, the battle of wills seems lost. Yet, I cling to my last hope: why not help just one person? This sends the beast reeling backwards with madness, shocked, and doubting his control.

I rise to my full stature, confident that I can help create one less victim. Now I have purpose, strong will, hope, and on this day, this hour, this minute, I choose recovery. No longer a victim of my fears, but an instrument of love.

I smiled at the beast as I looked in the mirror. I forgive you!

HIGHWAY TO SALVATION
George B.

If life's destination is death, then birth is the entrance to the toll road at mile marker zero. The price of the token is one's last breath and your soul.

I came out of the starting blocks. Clearly, there was no need for foster homes or adoption agencies to slow my pace. The first hurdle on the path was a father who used a cat-o-nine tails, metal-tipped braided leather, every drunken Saturday night, to punish my indiscretions he'd miss during the week. Dreams of perfect parents was a way to cope, until I ran away. The pathway of adolescence meandered its tortuous route and soon became a Boulevard with side streets named Cigarettes, Alcohol, Gangs, Sex, and Drugs, wayside banners rampant with opportunities, to succeed at failure.

Juvenile Court Judges and indolent parents pointed the way to castles of supreme beings they were too busy to attend. Revivalists in tents thumped their holy books, pounding the un-penitent with promises of fire and brimstone. In tongues, moved by some unseen spirit, they rolled onto the pulpit the body and blood, with promise of golden ducats to the pearly white gates at the end of the highway to heaven, offering a personal co-pilot for when I lost my way, some bearded fella by the name of Jesus ready to guide me, if only I called his name.

Determined to pilot my own course, the distracting Billboards offer easy access to side streets with names like Easy Women, Easier Money, and Free Booze just past the next bend. Fatal pot holes lay in the fast lane—Vietnam, Cambodia, Organized Crime, and Prison. Stopping to repair flat tires, temptation often diverts me. Forging on, another sign, but beyond the divide of the right path on the right for the righteous. The road to Salvation is a drag. I veer left at the fork, to Vegas, loveless marriage, and infidelity.

Exiting at Good Times, a glittering Harrah's Casino, no windows, no clocks; longing for eternity is easy. Free drinks with the turn of a card, every pleasure, a gift of the casino host. Money isn't money, the plastic chips come with a swipe of a plastic card. Plastic love with a polyethylene conscience. I'm trapped in the gridlock trying to get back to the highway until I finally call for "the co-pilot".

On the not so straight and narrow highway, hurtling toward my goal, the highway splits again. The unmarked choice was simple: go right, or veer to the left. The easy way is to the left, the Road to Perdition, where I could have it all; to the right, the road is hard, and the scenery boring.

A sinkhole fills the road: I am going too fast to slow down. Instinct demands that I drop down two gears and punch it. Floating over the sinkhole, I realize there is no way to avoid falling into the pit. The abyss is huge, filled with all my sins. My way is lost. I have shunned all the signs that pointed me to Salvation, the hedonistic pleasures of Perdition being such an easy choice.

But I must try a different route this time. I'll call one more time. He may be there.

THE INTRODUCTION
Bruce L.

I knew a man in prison, who told me a very long story. I think he was trying to teach me something, but I would not listen. He was showing me things, but I refused to look.

The story was about a man who came to prison with only two years to serve, a man who turned his sentence into more than seventeen. The man continued down a path of destruction, harming others, and in turn, himself. He was sent to the Security Housing Unit, where he spent six years.

During that time, the man asked himself, "Is this how I want to spend the rest of my life? Why have I hurt so many people? What have I become?" The answers to these questions demanded action. He committed treason, giving up on his old belief system, abandoning former gang affiliates and crime partners.

He made the decision to change his life, and to change his thinking. Changing his identity changed how he related to the world, and the world to him.

That someone I met in prison was me.

CAN A ROCK CEASE TO BE A ROCK?
Fernando L.

I rise from a dirty river, farmed fields, the smell of clean air, a losing basketball team, and politicians. These are the things that cradled me as a child, memories that have been suffocated by a new reality.

Hours turned to days and days to uneventful years, as I stepped off the bus into the bowels of another prison, endlessly depleting my morale. The sign above the door, "R & R" (refused and rejected), stands proud as if lit in neon, announcing to all that they're entering the next phase of this industrialized processing plant known as CDCR.

Intense reflection, combined with years of work in many self-help programs, taught me I could change. However, this was not always the case. My first 10 years were difficult. I was naïve and self destructive. I even nurtured those defects that got me into trouble, and that list grew.

Every morning I woke feeling like a person who had been discussed, argued about, demonized, marginalized, excluded from society, included in statistics, tried, transported, documented, fingerprinted, incarcerated, given a number, urine tested, swabbed, observed, and measured. This is how I was categorized; I was declared hopeless and irredeemable. As much as these labels hurt, they were the truth.

Hitting rock bottom was emasculating and treacherous, but a necessary step if I was to reclaim my life. I had to consciously decide to remove the denim and to clothe myself with self respect. I worked hard, struggling at times, but in the end, I felt a sense of purpose. I am grateful to the men and women who believed I could be more. I try to pay their kindness forward by becoming a source of inspiration to those around me.

THE HAIRCUT
Victor G.

Six years ago, in a drunken mist, I was perched on a chrome steel dayroom table. I hear, "Hey, today's haircut day." I was not up to the task, preferring to continue drowning myself in my cell-made wine, hoping each gulp would carry me away from harsh reality. Instead, I found myself back in my cell to cut my client's hair.

I got out a mirror, razors, combs, and loose razor blades and began shaving the side of his head, reviving the fade he'd been sporting for the past ten years. All the while, I kept eye contact to a minimum to avoid tribulations I might see behind those coffee-brown eyes.

But it was too late. Throughout the haircut I could sense his unease at my eyes exchanging glances with his. As I held up my mirror—made out a chip bag wrapped around the bottom of a plastic cup—to reflect the back of his head, our eyes locked.

I erupted. "How dare you look me in the eye after what you have cost me!" I am forever branded a murderer.

Thanks to you, gone is the sacred promise I made to my daughter and her mother—to always be there for them, leaving me with the guilt of failure and a sea of sadness, never knowing how much Marilyn has grown, wondering if my absence clouds her bright smile when asked, "Where's your dad?" Or whether her mom reaches out for my support, only to feel the grasp of my absence.

How dare you stand before me, drunk, knowing what I will forever miss. I don't ever want to see you again. Behind these walls is where I leave you, you damned beast! And here is where I begin to nurture into a man, that little boy you no longer hold captive.

BORN BAD?

Melvin Price

One day I'll die. I wont even have to try. I'll simply disappear right before your very eyes. So, while you still have me, enjoy the bad guy. The Pete Wentz of my friends, I'm the Fall Out Boy. I usually sided with my friends over my family. Instead of shooting a Spalding basketball or a nine millimeter, I was shooting for the Grammy's.

Age nine, my train to the awards got derailed, when an auntie of mine wanted to teach me how sex feels. That ended up breaking my heart, so I fixed it with pain pills. First the reds, then the blues, like a Pez dispenser. In my self portrait of the bad guy, I used my vomit to paint the picture.

I had hopes and dreams, just like you. I rooted for the Cops to catch the bad guys, too.

Then things switched. Man, life is a bitch. And her moms is a jail, her grandson's a jail cell, the rest of her relatives are hoping you fail. Opinions are like bad hair days; everybody has one. We all know at least one bad guy, we just don't know how he became one. I was a cute kid—chubby cheeks, grandma's favorite. Now I'm F37541, and my hope is fading. Silver Bic razor to my wrist, is my life worth saving?

When I feel this way my sweat drips dark red. Last night I snuggled with the devil in bed; afterword, we had pillow talk; this is what he said: "People greater than you die everyday. At their funerals, folks say this and that, then forget about them in six months flat, ten months max, and that ratio is cut in half, especially if you're black."

Then, a montage played of every cruel teacher, every wavy-haired girl that ignored me in the bleachers, every time I was profiled due to my bad-guy features. There's another opinion but who wants to hear that? Because hey, life is great unless you were born bad.

CLINK CLINK
Julian V.

Boom, Boom, a man dies. Clink- clink, the cuffs go on. Clink, Clink, the cuffs come off. I'm 16 years old and in Central Juvenile Hall. I walk into the block and the first words I hear, "Hey fool, where are you from? F--- your barrio, punk. You ain't nothing." Clink, Clink, I'm in the Big House now. Walking the yard, Bonaroo Down, head held high, flagging my colors, a Q-vo here and there.

I hear the brown magic lady calling. She doesn't care what flag I'm riding, only that I'm faithful to her. She sings to me and dances inside. I'm enchanted by her embrace, yet she is toxic.

Boom-Boom. "Get down!" Clink, Clink, I'm in the SHU. Light's on, chow time. "One in the front, one in the back. Pick up your trays." Clink, Clink, I'm in the Big House, again. Ring-Ring, "Mama, Mama, send me some money—please."

Knock, knock, "Shotgun, we need to talk." Smell of dead fish coming from the chow hall is a bad omen. My stomach turns, as the conversation I was dreading is now in my face. "Shotgun, we need something done. He needs to be taken out in a box!"

I was reminded of a promise I had made to never shed blood with these hands. "Officer I don't want to hurt anyone or myself anymore. I can't stay here." Clink, Clink, you're SNY now [Sensitive Needs Yard, formerly known as the "Protection Unit"], inmate. There's no turning back.

I fall asleep and awake to a whisper "Julian, I'm calling you." "Yes, father?" He tells me, "today is your first day. "

THE DAY MY LIFE CHANGED
Nicholas F.

The dining hall a familiar sight, the foul smell of week-old coffee hovers. Convicts greet each other with smiles, as the meeting is called to order. Introductions are made, spiritual principles discussed. I have no clue as to what this topic's about. I don't read the Bible. The facilitator, an old salt-and-pepper-haired Uso, white push-broom stache, reminds me of the walrus in the Chilly Willy cartoon. There's a mean look to him, always so serious, but I listen to his message. He talks about exchanging bad for good, changing from dishonest to honest. I begin to understand spiritual principles.

A big-headed guy stands and begins to share. He looks like blockhead Charlie Brown. Another positive message I embrace as he discusses life-changing experiences.

All I wanted was my Chrono for the parole board in May, not to hear a bunch of war stories. I was a hard-core gang banger.

His message is powerful, though, hitting home with me. Hearing others share shows me they're as messed up as me. It is all starting to sink in, and I'm feeling this group. It turns out the walrus isn't such a bad guy after all; that also goes for blockhead.

My first day at CGA changed my life completely, waking me from a fog. And I know I'll be a part of this for the rest of my life.

WITHIN THE MINORITY
Kevin H.

Fear and worry debilitated the blue-eyed teenager as he sought refuge within the Folsom dungeon. Lighting streaks of blood spattered his face as he stared at the ancient gun towers and bullet-riddled granite walls.

Never in his childhood did the young man envision that life could turn out this way, with the key to liberty chucked beyond reach. Insecurities, excessive concern with what others thought, and a need to impress spawned senselessly bad decisions. A lifetime of shame and ridicule stained the upbringing of a loner whose life revolved around a can of Chef Boyardee raviolis and hand-me-downs from the local thrift shop. His failures in school and loneliness were masked by addiction and crime.

Drowned in delusion and seeking to impress, he bolstered his lack of confidence with self-aggrandizing lies and violence. Devastation and death were imminent: a rippling undertow consumed those in his wake.

…Locked away within layers of false bravado, my icy stare sizes them up. "What's up homeboy?" slips through my quivering lips, to someone I don't know, yet call a brother. I wonder what his thoughts are, as I don my prison toughness, assuring that I belong.

After decades of seclusion, I look back to discover where everything went wrong. No longer needing the labels of the masses or satisfied with merely going with the flow, I grasp a new identity, characterized by confidence, truth, and compassion. Positive roots take hold, and scars began to fade as a new life begins, within the minority.

TREASURE CHEST
Frank N.

Nuestra Señora De Atocha was a Spanish galleon that sank off the coast of Florida in 1622 while returning to Spain from America. It carried stolen goods.

Native American Land was being conquered and pillaged. The huge conquistadors with their metal amour and massive swords must have looked liked Gods emerging from the sea. Native tribes were in awe, offering food and gifts to the giants, including jewelry made of rust-resistant metal. Seeing such splendor, the Spaniards' greed erupted in a campaign of savagery and looting. Satiated, they loaded their ship with boundless treasures and set course for home.

Mother Nature had other plans. She lashed out violently, sinking the Nuestra Señora and her bounty.

Selfishly, I, too, was a ship in search of lands to conquer. Lust and greed consumed me. The streets were my oceans. Destruction powered my sails. My moral compass shattered, I had no sense of direction. I steered directly into the path of the merciless and powerful Hurricane Addiction. I was no match; there was no turning back. Crashing waves pounded my soul. Disoriented, I lost control.

Looking out across the crashing waves, I saw the Angel of Death drawing near. His eyes were pits of blackness, his face and hands skeleton-like. I panicked, covering my head with trembling hands, in anticipation of my doom.

With what little strength I had left, I made a desperate plea to God to save my life. Immediately, the winds calmed. Lightening and thunder ceased. Peaceful bliss replaced the violent storm. I opened my eyes: the Angel of Death was gone. I saw a magnificent light entering my chest, where my dark heart had been replaced by precious jewels of human redemption—love, integrity, honesty, and courage.

REFLECTIONS
Julian V.

Mirror, mirror, on the wall, who is the prettiest of them all? Our eyes meet; this is mental warfare. If I blink he wins and kicks me in the nads, or jabs me in the throat, or hits me where it really hurts. Damn, I blinked. "It's definitely never you, heavy fats," the mirror says. That was one of the many stinging nick names the mirror used.

I've always had problems with my weight, my looks, the way I speak, and my lack of education. I had no self esteem or confidence. I didn't even like myself most of the time. I've had a few relationships while I was in prison. I never really understood what those women saw in me. God forgive me, but at that time I thought those women were crazy, especially for being with someone like me. They must have been mental. God bless their little hearts for putting up with me and leaving.

When they did, it took professional help and a lot of hard work to find the root of my problems. Putting such a broken, insecure man back together takes time.

I've learned two very important things. First, surrender! There are things beyond our control. I surrendered myself to my God, with all my shortcomings. Second, forgive! Healing can begin only after you forgive yourself—and others. In time, I have built strength and character where I had little. I shine like a new star. I walk with a smile, head held high. I feel like a new man.

Those insecurities? I laugh at them now. I lost some weight, changed the way I speak and think, and have tried to educate myself. "Who says you can't teach an old dog new tricks?" With hard work and my new family standing firmly behind me, I can now walk up to that old mirror with confidence.

Having that big smile on my face, I ask it, "mirror, mirror, on the wall, who is *now* the prettiest of them all?" "Dude, it's still not you!"

ISSUES, ISSUES, ISSUES
Melvin P.

I still wear my skateboard shoes, even though they hurt my feet. I'm getting older, but I refuse to agree. Orthopedic shoes just aren't cool. How many girls hitting the club this week in cute little pumps that hurt their feet agree with me? Now tell me that ain't insecure.

Am I going to have to find a Gwyneth Paltrow of my own before I can speak purely—beautiful, and sincere—like every lyric in Coldplay's Parachute album? The "Mooch" told me "The key to honesty is to stop telling lies, and not all at once, just one lie at a time."

But situations vary, like shifting sand; each person is different from Woman to Man. So, instead of keeping it real, I just keep it as real as I can.

Melvin's got issues, and here are a few: I'm anti-social, but fear being alone too. I use sarcasm as a weapon. I laugh to keep from crying. I'm afraid of hell, but not afraid of dying.

There's someone out there right now thinking they're better than me, because they got that Ryan Gosling six pack, and no felonies. But who am I to judge? I probably think I'm better then you, because I can play Stairway to Heaven, and Purple Haze, too.

Right now I'm on the rebound of a divorcee. I told her "You want to make your ex-husband really mad? Then start dating me." My friends say I am selling myself short, "Any woman would be lucky to have me." I smile like I'm in the court room, nod my head and agree. But inwardly I disagree because of my insecurity.

I've got stretch marks, tattoos, and scars on my face. The Honorable Long Beach City Judge told me "The streets without me are a much safer place." Sticks and stones break bones, but words hurt much more. I built a wall made of money to block out the insecure.

Five mirrors in my room, so I can see how I look. I minimize everything that made me a crook. I refuse to go shopping without at least $25.00 dollars on my books. I'm way too insecure to get caught eatin' just my state lunch.

My friends are all happy with their comfortable lives, they go shopping at Wal-mart with their comfortable wives. And me, I have no one, but pretend its all right. I'm too insecure to let my friends know how I feel inside.

GOOD ENOUGH
Cesar L.

My turn inches closer and closer, as one more seat becomes vacant. An intense worry threatens what confidence I've built toward knowing what I'm about. I inhale deeply, wondering how long this fit of apprehension will last this time. "They won't like you," "You're too messed up," "You won't be accepted." Taunting demons jest and jeer about my worth.

Refuge in the blissful seclusion of the mind-numbing spoon, quart, or gang is no longer an option. The years of opiate-induced nods, pruno stupors, and adrenaline-juiced fights mask the memories of this young man, now lost in the loneliness of the mess I'd made of my life.

Some of those I've known would attest to the validity of those taunts about my shortcomings. But few ever looked beyond my protective mask to see my pain-filled eyes and wounded soul. Those who dared were soon rejected, lest they, too, find fault. So deep ran my scars of failure.

Now, as I delve into the work of rebuilding, I know I must lay a firm foundation, knowing full well that struggles are sure to come. One seat closer. I readjust my mental armor, preparing for the battle each step is sure to present.

A resounding clap announces the finish of my predecessor and the focal point of my struggles. Step by step I reach for the podium. Scared and worried, I look up and begin the business of subduing my insecurity about not being good enough. "Hi, I'm Cesar, I'm an addict, an alcoholic, and a gang dropout. Thank you for letting me share."

"DON'T FEED THE MONKEYS"
Fernando L.

When you all signed up to come to the zoo, you were told not to feed the monkeys. You can't feed them praise, or come in contact with them, and certainly, don't talk to them about anything other than their essays.

So how does Curious George feel? Who truly is benefiting from the watching—those being watched, or those doing the watching? This monkey wonders, "Is this class nothing more than a social experiment designed to appear to be a writing class when, in actuality, the students are here to observe and listen to the heart beat of the underworld?" Oh, how sad and pathetic we must sound. Or are the monkeys just playing around, hoping to gain sympathy from the onlookers? As they maintain a safe distance from behind the protective guard tables, one can only guess.

I take a deep breath and reel in my insecurity to a more manageable level. It doesn't matter what these kids are here for; what matters is what am I here for. So, as I put pen to paper, I become thankful for Paul and Lori because they're providing me with a different opportunity to get to know myself. Life slowly fades back to blue.

OLD FRIEND
Tyrone H.

Friends go and come, some waiting anxiously to be gone again. Some leave behind the dusty, sour taste of a hung-over mouth. Others leave lasting & joyous memories we'll carry with us. I once had a friend who'd do anything for me. All I had to do was ask, and he'd provide. In fact, most of his days were spent helping others in the community any way he could.

Much older than me, he made a point of being available when I came calling. As my life became more troubled, I'd call on the old man for help. He always came through—be it posting my bail or sending someone to rescue me in a pinch. I never thanked him, nor showed appreciation for all he'd done, and eventually turned my back on him. Yet I never forgot the Bible-Packing old man, sharing his wisdom about the less-traveled road.

Subtle as a tsunami and devastating as the darkest dark, my life took dramatic turns for the worse. The hold-your-breath fear of snaking through a window was replaced by a vulture-like thirst for blood. My days slowly waltzed into decades, as I danced on blood-stained waves of destruction, eventually landing me in prison.

Looking around my cell, I saw all the creature comforts allowed—TV, radio, soups, and sodas. For prison, I had stuff; but with all these things, my soul was empty. I thought of the things my old friend said and his promise to be there.

With the tears of a broken man, I dropped to my knees and prayed, calling out to my old friend. As promised, he answered my call, rejoicing to welcome the Prodigal Son back home.

GRANTED
Kevin H.

Prison glass shattered by the blue-eyed, angelic-cloaked succubus, her intoxicating pleasures branded with a searing prod. Venus and Mars on a collision course with a blood-dipped dagger inscribed "epiphany." Vows, filled with lies of "for better or worse," were empty sacraments flung to the wind.

A liar in need, now accused, shielded her truth with a mask of deception. I, thought unsuitable by the masses—and she, the bandwagon renegade—was condemned to a razor wire abyss.

Fueled by her forked tongue of flame was Liberty, while hobbled with years of torment was the Light of Promise. Letters of conscience seeking forgiveness from infidelity were laced with trip wires of failure, "I'm so sorry." Mine fields of "Wish you luck" came next.

The tentacles of serenity entangled me with a ribbon of completion. As I stood before the governor's chosen, my plea for life ended with a verdict of suitability, "GRANTED" stamped across the parchment.

Through seeds of faith, the molten magma of captivity cooled, with deception, anger, fear, seclusion, and abandonment no longer the magnetic storm of blue-orb debilitation. Amazed at the vast possibilities of my future, the chains of bondage faded against a loveless past.

BE GONE!
Spencer B.

I lie chained in the depths of a dark pit. I do not know why I do this to myself. It's an unexplainable feeling. I cry out as the walls close in on me. Its voice keeps getting clearer. I often wish it would die. "I know you for what you are: you are not a friend. You are a contagious disease of bad deeds and negativity, but for some reason, I haven't been able to get rid of you after all we've been through." Catch and release, hooked as a fish, always being reeled back to you, only to be skinned of hope and cooked in your poison. Loath to look at your face, I hate myself all the more because the face I see is mine.

THE BODY
Patrick A.

The 12-step meeting already in progress, I enter the small prison chapel to slide into the first available seat. Fifty of us gather here every week, most serving life sentences, to understand the fears and insecurities that allowed us to kill and, equally important, to learn a better way of living.

I listened to a man speaking from the front of the room, his tattooed arms pounding the wooden podium. "After 30 years in prison, I've served enough time behind bars," each word launching splinters of selfishness. "I deserve to go home," he demanded, before turning the battered podium over to the next man.

Enticed by my own sense of deservedness, my Attention Deficit Disorder had led me from one rabbit hole to the next, as I neatly piled my shiny jailhouse accomplishments upon a scale of righteousness—College degree, youth mentor, a slew of self-help accolades. I am a far cry from the teenager who, in the neon light of a local Mom and Pops market, stood lookout amongst discount beer posters while, inside, a man bled to death, robbed of his life.

Too easily, I marvel at the person I've become. That is, until I place the body on the balance. No matter how gentle I am, he slams the scales down, firing all my shininess to the stars, as his body lands at my feet.

Twenty years in prison inches me forward in my seat, as I plant my face in palms grown atop elbows that seem rooted in my knees; "deservedness" ricochets between my ears and slows to swirl upon my tongue. In a hushed whisper, the word drops. My eyes follow, watching the word I dare not say turn red as it splashes off my tennies, as shotgun pellets are flung violently across the body's bright, white shirt.

Barely understanding, I yank a handkerchief from my pocket and apologize before blotting the red stains pumping from his chest. "I know, I know," I say to the body at my feet, "Deserve?...What the hell am I thinking?"

Pools of burgundy seep from his back and run across the linoleum, eating the floor behind the cash register. Realizing the futility, I suggest, "Come, old friend. Why don't we get out of here?" Silently, he agrees.

Kneeling, I tenderly lift him from the cold market floor to place him lovingly over my shoulders. Together we trudge on, forward in recovery, but never deserving.

KALEIDOSCOPE
Tyrone H.

I live in a kaleidoscope of ever-changing masks and attitudes, one for every occasion, each carrying its own trademark of anguish and confusion. "Who am I?" I often muse, my confusion cutting through me like shards of glass.

When I am afraid, it silently screams, "Show no fear!" When I am happy and smiling, it reminds me, "Show no weakness." Everywhere I look, it's there watching me, ready to pounce. I wear one to hide the one I wear, layer upon layer.

I have no idea who I am. I pretend to be who I am not, the mask of deception fortifying the falsehoods I've come to believe in— hate, betrayal, distrust, skepticism and isolation. It tells me I hate what I love and I love what I hate.

The kaleidoscope gathers speed as it spins, blinding and confusing. Overwhelmed, I find strength to look away, to find reality, to witness the collateral damage and destruction left behind.

How many masks did I have? I see the mask of, "I don't give a fuck," next to drug-addicted parents, a father I couldn't cry for when he died, a mother reduced to a homeless bag lady. I pretended not to care as I drove by her.

I see the mask of, "I'm better off without you," as I put distance between myself and family, desperately wanting to be a part of the whole, but not knowing how. I isolated myself, turning my back on those who cared for me.

I see the mask of, "You're better off without me," the bullshit I told myself about my child. I was never there for him as he grew up, doing my part to perpetuate the vicious cycle of neglect and abandonment. I left the carnage of so many relationships in my wake. Why? Because I was afraid to be who I was—the real me.

As each mask is erased, layer after layer, I see the pain I have caused. Had I let my love show, my child would have grown up knowing he had a loving father. Had I shown regard for human life, Tymon wouldn't have suffered my attempt to take his life or those of countless victims before him.

In the winter of 2003, as I lay shivering on my hard bunk in Salinas Valley State Prison, the kaleidoscope came to a grinding halt when I prayed to God for help. "Help me to overcome this person I am not and restore me to the person I want to be." My body convulsed from emotions long suppressed, and I saw clearly the persons of my past—and future.

Removing my masks of deception has been painstaking. I make every attempt to reverse the damage I caused to my victims and myself. Being open and honest, expressing discomfort, and voicing my opinion, I realize there's no shame or weakness in asking for help or offering forgiveness.

My kaleidoscope now emits beautiful and colorful lights of kindness, joy, happiness, service, confidence, and a true love of life, self, and others.

ARMY OF THE PHOENIX
Manuel J.

When I open my eyes every morning, I make a commitment. I commit to my recovery by remembering that today will be a battle against the skeleton army of my past, led by a vicious General named Anger, his right hand man, the impetuous and merciless Lieutenant Dishonesty—a cunning, oily-tongued demon— and Sergeant Insecurity, who whispers in the ears of the battalion.

This is the opposition I face day in, day out. They've embedded themselves deep in the trenches of my soul. But also I have my own army, and a strategy. I have kindness, which I use like a pair of binoculars, to spot and evade the enemy. When I see the vicious General, I redirect my path. When I spot his lackeys, I have artillery: I can never destroy them, but I can fend them off. A firefight of wills, my recovery is an Armageddon of its own. Angels versus demons. Yin versus Yang. Clash of the Titans. When I close my eyes before I sleep, I whisper poetry to my Army of Angels. I want to thank them for defending me.

As I rest, I smile because once again, my battle was won. One day closer to defeating my flaws and defects, my insecurities, my dishonesty, my selfishness and irresponsibility. Yes, I fight them all. I won the battle today, but not the war, because as I tend to my platoon and mend their wounds, my flaws and defects are burying land mines to trip us up. They're in the war room drawing up plans.

I, too, have sustained wounds. I wear them like a badge of courage. Crimson ribbons caress my skin; their warmth reminds me I'm alive. But this was the choice of choices. This is the main event I signed on for—David versus Goliath, King Kong against Godzilla— my determination to rebuild the bridges I have destroyed; to re- assemble myself as a better man, a human being with empathy, patience, and understanding. My aim is to rise from the ashes of a destroyed temple.

Clawing my way from beneath the scattered rubble, I emerge as a Phoenix, spreading my wings, flapping my fiery feathers with every molecule of my existence. I will fly high with joy and victory. I've only begun. This is merely the sixth step on a twisting stairway to the heavens. My destination is the top, the Mount Olympus of recovery.

RESURRECTION
Craig H.

"**D**on't call me Trigger," I said, pounding my finger into the stainless steel table top with emphasis, "My name is Craig." My old friend, from what seemed a past life, didn't understand the significance of my statement. Hell, abstract concepts of identity politics, I barely understood it myself.

Trigger, as I'd been known on the streets of Santa Ana, was a thug who never backed down, gun-toting, quick-on-the-draw, my chrome 45 in your face, demanding respect as you crapped your pants. Trigger is who I became when I shot Craig in the face and turned my back on love.

For years I'd sought my native roots. The day I walked over to the Native American sweat lodge at RJ Donovan, the Indian Brothers had just come out of ceremony; the aroma of wood smoke and burnt sage thick on their bodies. Offering my hand, I introduced myself as "Trigger."

The sweat leader openly held my eyes as we shook hands-native style. Without letting go, he asked, "What is your real name?" Taken back by what I considered an odd question, I answered "Craig," without thinking. "Good," he said, giving me an intense, lasting stare. Before releasing me, he asked in a manner more like a command than a request, "Why don't you try that? It's a strong name." That was the day the proud and responsible man who my loving grandmother raised was resurrected.

50-YEAR-OLD TEENAGER
Oscar G.

I stare at the wrinkles. Tattoos decorate his face and run down his neck, red and green covering 80 percent of his body. "Yo, what's crack-a-lakin boyee?" he says. His more than140 seasons of being caged is a clear qualifier of triple 0.6 status.

Even in his fifties, he still acts like a teen; but that's what happens when you've been locked-up since 18. He finished a set of push-ups off the iron bars and pounded his chest growling "Check out the hood." We jogged a few laps while he complained about an overdue parole date.

"I'm ready to go," he whined. But I don't think even he believed himself. I look at the crows feet again, this time imagining myself in his tennies. Will I end up the same? Will I be content being a yard bum and complaining to some youngster? Could I endure 30 years of let-downs, separations, reunions, and more separations? And will it take me three decades to come to my senses and change my life?

FIRE
Patrick A.

The Big Indian, that's what my grandmother called him. My great-grandfather was born a New Mexico Apache in 1904, along the Rio Grande. At 6'7" and broad as a bull buffalo, he was the biggest Indian I knew. He'd moved his family to California after the Great War to build the railroad through the San Gabriel Valley. I was barely five and stood only as tall as his thigh.

I can still see him standing next to his old Chevy pick-up, dented and spotted with grey primer like an Appaloosa pony. Long braids of hair hung from below a black Quaker hat. His watch was fastened to a wide leather wristband that complemented a thick silver and turquoise ring. A maduro leaf cigarette that he called a cigaro hung from between his beefy fingers.

Great-grandad and I had caught the matinee after spending the morning fishing. Hopping back into the truck, he was about to push the ignition, when, thinking of the movie, I asked, "Why did Bambi's home have to burn when the hunters came?" Hesitating, finger on the button, he sank back against the bench seat without turning over the engine. He pulled meditatively on his cigaro and gazed into the distance, to a far off time that only old folks can see.

I began to wonder if he'd forgotten I was there, when he exhaled a thick plume of smoke. Then, shaking his head, he told me it didn't. Another long drag, a puff of smoke and a year seemed to pass before he leaned toward the dashboard and pushed the button labeled "start."

I pondered the stoic answer as we drove in silence. The old pony carried us down the long, dusty driveway of our home. Gravel popped and crunched under the worn tires as we glided to a stop. While the motor kicked, knocked, and rattled its death-song, I wondered aloud, "If it didn't have to, then why did it burn?" He glared with steely eyes that cut my soul, sliced it in half.

It was not until he spoke that I understood that what I had perceived as hostility was actually the anguish of the Redman. How could I comprehend that a leathery, crevasse-faced Indian would view Bambi from a perspective beyond my own? "Did you see any Indians in that picture show?" Before I could answer he replied,

"Son, our people have been the protectors of Mother Earth from before-before. The hunters came to our home, too. We were driven like cattle, flung from the land and rubbed out. There are no more protectors." It seemed like an eternity as he reflected on his words.

Gathering his thoughts, he continued softly, "When I was your age, I served as an assistant to the Fire-Keeper during the Great Sweat Ceremonies. This was the job of the children. We were taught to respect the fire; we learned its dance. Fire lives: it breathes, consumes, destroys, and gives life. When I grew to a young man, before the war came, I was a firefighter. The reservation had the best firefighters, because we respected the fire."

"It is our job to protect Mother Earth. The Creator taught the Ancient Ones and our elders have passed those teachings to us. Just as I have told you stories of Coyote, White Painted Woman, and of Creation, it will be your job to teach your children." I said nothing as we sat there as he finished his cigaro. I decided then I would become a fireman. I would protect our home and Bambi's forest.

Eight winters had gone since my great-grandpa's passing. I was thirteen-years-old as I walked towards a fork in the road. The small firehouse was along the route to my new school, but this was the first time I saw anyone out front.

Filled with anxiety, I worked up the courage to speak, "Excuse me, sir. How can I become a fireman?" He was bent over, busy laying out fire hoses along the cement driveway when I spoke. He knelt down and looked up in my direction. The sun shone over my shoulder, so he cocked his head to the side to escape its rays. His moustache was trimmed military style, allowing me to see his teeth when his upper lip rose, and he squinted.

Then, he stood, tucking his thumbs into the waistband of his dark blue work pants. His chest expanded with air under his firefighter t-shirt, and I held my breath in expectation. "Well," he exhaled, looking down at me, "the most important thing is do well in school and get good grades."

I hung on every word, but my years of struggling in school flooded my mind. I worked harder than any of my classmates, and still, I failed miserably. I tried so hard—and failed—to earn good grades that I had come to believe the other kids who called me stupid. I seemed incapable of doing well in school. The impossible would be required if I were to be like my great-gramps. I crumbled. I thanked him politely before heading down the road. I ditched school and never looked back.

Many moons have passed since giving up on my firehouse dream. Today I am an Industrial Maintenance worker who races up ladders whenever an alarm sounds, drops into confined spaces, and runs from one crisis to another. More importantly, I am able to defuse explosive frustration, mediate between raging actions, and gently tamp down someone's smoldering anger. I have built myself into a new man after laying waste to the insecure, broken child who entered prison nearly twenty years ago. I have learned that I don't have to ride on a bright red truck with bells a-ringing to put out fires.

PART 7. NEW BEGINNINGS

We must become the change we wish to see in the world.

- Mahatma Ghandi

WONDERLAND
Jorge R.

I t was a hot, sunny day in late July. Proud parents and anxious grads paraded down the smooth, wide roads of a place called Wonderland, where students came to mark their intellectual advancement. Master's, MD's, and Ph.D's peppered the compound, all bragging about their accomplishments. I preferred silence, blocking out the celebrating chatter, as I drank in my moment of success.

Today I am no longer a regular man, but a member of an intellectual society. My struggling days and dedication finally paid off. After today, life will be much easier. With so many prestigious job offers, I'll be able to enjoy the fruits of my hard work.

Soaked with sweat, I wake up on a hard, small concrete slab, encased in steeled doors, to a scream of, "Turn on your lights; it's chow time!" With an ache in my heart, I realize I wasn't in Wonderland, and I hadn't earned a Master's degree—or any degree. It was just another fantasy of my subconscious. Many times I have dreamed; but for the first time, it was not of a chaotic life.

PATRICIA
Tyrone H.

Walking through the door, I search for my love. Stomach trembling anxiously, I am, once again, transformed into a nervous bundle of teenaged imperfections. Only she makes me feel this way.

Excitement sends a face-breaking smile to my lips as I spot her in the visiting room. Disguised as goose bumps, happiness does its thrilling dance across my body.

I maneuver through the small room. As if in a trance, I make my way into her arms. We are alone on a rapturous island, overgrown with flowers bearing the names "Elation," "Ecstasy," and "Euphoria".

Looking into her enthusiastic green eyes brimming in love, I know joy. The pure serenity of our love is my greatest joy!

DEAR SISTER
Bernie F.

Dear Sister Janet,
I was deeply touched by your response to my life story. Lydia's letter expressed your compassion. Your lifelong dedication to fighting the good fight, your willingness to go beyond name and face of all those undesirable cases, your determination to dig through the rubbish left by earthquakes at the epicenter of our lives, makes you a blessing. You are a gift from God to all of humanity. You are an inspiration to all who lacked a teacher in the field of compassion; for all who continue to stumble through ignorance in desperate search of meaning in life.

As I read Lydia's words, I felt the genuine love and admiration she has for you. It resonates throughout her letter. Your love and passion is so powerful, it reaches those of us thousands of miles away, hidden from civilization. Though I'm only beginning to know you, it is not difficult to see why you have such a strong affect on people. Yours is the real Midas Touch: where Midas could only enrich the superficial aspect of an object by turning it to gold, you create gold mines within the heart and soul of each life you touch.

The riches you share will endure until the end of time. Our desolate land will again be a rich field of crops because of the seeds you have planted in our hearts. You are God's green thumb tending gently to His garden.

I know it's discouraging, disheartening even, when stories of people like me seem never-ending. I know you can't physically liberate everyone, but I do know your efforts will liberate the hearts, minds, and spirits of men and women in places like these. Most often, it is the prison we create within ourselves that causes the most pain. If we can't free ourselves from that, it won't matter where we spend our lives. We'll always be miserable.

You are making a difference in how I perceive my world. Your story has taught me to trust and believe in the goodness of the human spirit. You give the world hope. Further, I suspect there is so much goodness in all of humanity that, eventually, the fighters of the good fight will prevail.

SKITTLES
Johnny S.

As I enter the visiting room, I find my wife's face awash with concern. My heart begins pounding the inner cavity of my chest—thump, thump, thump; something is amiss.

I Hold my wife tightly, our passionate kiss over in seconds. She whispered, "Our son has Attention Deficit Disorder, and the colors yellow and orange hurt his eyes." Thunderstruck, I turn to my nine-year-old in disbelief, as he stands patiently waiting for his turn of hugs and kisses.

I squat eye-level to my son, his little arms quickly encircling my neck. A tight embrace was his way of saying "Pick me up dad," which was often. Lifting him up, I think, "What the hell does a school teacher and school doctor know, anyway?" "I love you more than anybody, Dad," he whispers in my ear. Flooded with rage, my inner voice screams, "Fuck that school!" My boy popping ADD meds is out of the question.

After dropping a bag of Skittles before my spoiled son, I watch as he meticulously separates them by color; red, blue, orange, yellow. Suddenly, I am no longer angry, but afraid for my son, being so young yet so skilled in the art of deception. Fabricating a story to fool his teacher, his school doctor, and his mom to escape schoolwork could not be my son. It screamed, "Master Manipulator!"

Cupping my hand over the yellow and orange piles, I pretend to remove them. I await my spoiled son's reaction to losing half his Skittles. I innocently ask, "Oh, but don't those yellow and orange Skittles hurt your eyes?" Caught in the web of his own lies, his eyes gape with shotgun understanding.

Later, he admitted being bored with class and no longer wanted to attend school. Recounting my own youth, those fading memories of yesterday, how could I be upset with my little big-boy for being me? Trapped between parental responsibility and my own disdain for school, I promised my son that we would attend together—him on the outside, me on the inside.

On June 3, 2005, I received an invitation to attend a celebration honoring those, including me, who had recently graduated. Feeling I hadn't really accomplished anything, I declined to go pick up a sheet of paper that really meant nothing to me. A week later, I received a card from my son congratulating me on successfully completing my GED.

"To my Dad, You did great! I am very proud of you! Love, Rueben." It was only then that I realized my accomplishment. His card is my GED and it means the world to me.

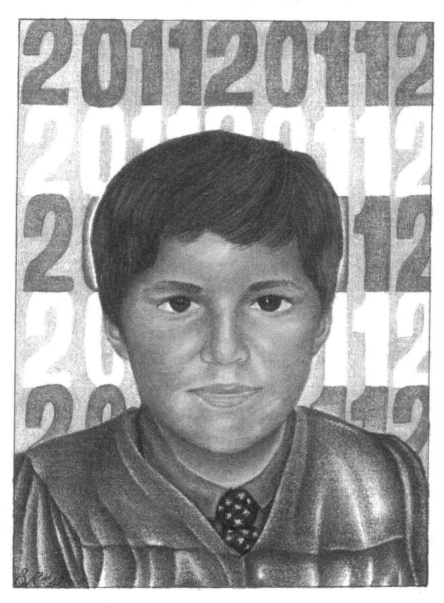

VOICE OF REASON
Craig H.

He introduced me to integrity, teaching me that those who are sincere can make a difference. Through open-mindedness, I could gain understanding and a transformation of character that would set me free.

We were of markedly different ages, yet I heard and understood his message. "Nobody can force you to change, for the decision is yours and yours alone." I was familiar with this old saying, but I had never taken it to heart. So, why now? I recalled times in my cell when I'd scoured every inch of the concrete walls with my eyes, looking for answers. I guess I didn't know it all.

I began seeking solutions to my destructive behavior. It had angered me to speak of my past or to be asked to admit fault, something that had caused my grandmother not to speak to me. Abandonment by my father added to my bitterness, selfishness and, ultimately, my fear of failure.

Trudging this old path, I was now shown a better way. Leading by example, he helped me to understand that change is possible. Grateful for our seemingly random meeting and for his commitment, integrity and compassion, I thank my friend, Sal.

CTRL + N
Jojo D.

From the wrong side of a county jail visiting booth, I peer into my father's red-rimmed eyes. He'd just learned that both his boys stood accused of murder. Looking deeper, I notice something different about the distant mask normally blanketing his face—sorrow. Seething, I thought, "What the hell *are* you doing here?"

All my life I had sought my father's affection, while his indifference burned black holes in my soul. No bed-time stories, no goodnight kisses. The more he pulled away, the more I rebelled. Anger became my guardian, crime, my ally. Smiles twisted into snarls.

Placing the cold visiting booth phone to my ear, fearful emotions roar, "I hate you!" But my lips too weak to voice the truth, the words crumble in my throat.

His distant glare softens as he reaches tentatively across the void to lay comfort on my shoulder. The attention I had longed for gushed through his tears, "I love you, son."

Doubt and fear battle in my gut while the possibility of forgiveness gnaws at my chest. Salt rocks, held back since youth, tumble down my cheek and shatter upon the floor.

Love no longer barred by resentment, the red-eyed stranger places his palm against the finger-stained window separating us, and the joyful boy of decades ago does the same, foraging a bond stronger than welded steel. A new beginning, a new friendship, a new chapter.

MOTHER
Eric O.

On October 8, 1954, an amazing woman was born. Strong and virtuous, she would become the backbone of our entire family. Working two jobs, she came home to barely sleep then leave again; never turning away family or friends in need of a place to stay; always reaching in her purse to drop money into the old weathered hats of the homeless; crossing herself in the name of the Father, Son, and Holy Spirit whenever she passed a Catholic Church or cemetery; and ever gentle raising her children.

Instead of gifts or money to acknowledge my accomplishments, she would take me to a park overlooking the city to breathe fresh air, climb trees, and watch boats sail under the Coronado bridge or to a favorite spot, La Jolla Cove, to watch the dark blue waves crash, vibrating the jagged rocks that form the cliffs.

Our life was not perfect, in fact, often hard; but through it all, I was warm, full, and had a roof over my head.

No matter how many times I say I'm sorry and explain it's not her fault, I see in her eyes the sadness and pain I've caused. It turns my stomach to know I've caused my mom so much guilt. Every night I ask God to lift her guilt and replace it with love and joy.

Watching my mom and nine-year-old daughter play, I see the sadness and pain disappear. The high-pitched laugh of my daughter echoes through the visiting room as my mom grabs to tickle her, to play with her, to love her. There's no question that little girl belongs to my mom, nine years old, still falling asleep in Abuela's arms, as my mom brushes away the hair from her face and smiles at me. I pray that somehow, even in some small way, this can make up for some of the pain I've caused.

MIJO QUERIDO
Joe A.

As he reached out to hold my hand, his brown eyes came alive. He smiled the words, "Mijo Querido" (My Dear Son). In disbelief, my brother asked him if he knew who I was. As if offended by the question, he insisted, "Claro pendejo, that's my son, Jose." We spent the next two hours listening to him recount stories of my youth.

I know love, because in that hot, crowded prison visiting room, a father's love for his son kicked Alzheimer's ugly ass.

GOD'S MIRACLE
Oscar M.

The erosion of years turns to decades. They crumble to the touch. January 20, 2009, the horror of a monotonous life yells "tic-toc, tic-toc." The concrete walls tighten their grip. I have trouble breathing.

4:00am—the floor is very cold, its iciness biting deep into my knees. My chest leans on the bunk's long metal support. My elbows are on my mattress as if it were a table. Hands to face, I reverently bow my head. I cry out in desperation, feeling more like a mouse than a man. Today, I am desperate for the warmth of intimacy! God, please, let me hear your voice.

My quiet prayer is no longer quiet! I hear in my own voice the word "soon!" I must be tripping. I ignore what I've heard and rush into more prayer. But something doesn't feel quite right. I tell myself, "Ask God another question. Surely he won't answer you a second time, and you'll be off the hook."

A little cocky, as if trying to derail God's plan, I ask, "How long must I wait, Lord?" I hear the voice reply, "Three days." Now I'm looking for an excuse and a fast way out. Frustrated, I ask the Lord, "And for what purpose must I wait?"

I felt a thundering voice; different from the first two. "Are three days too much for answered prayer, for healing? Would you not give everything for the mother of your children to love me? Is this not worth the wait?"

Rapidly, everything fell into place. It wasn't about me at all. On the last morning, 3:00am, I struggled: sleep was evasive. With all the love that I could muster, I started praying for Margaret. As I thought of her, my heart filled with warmth. Sadly, I started feeling empty and alone. My spirit yearned to hold her in my arms. I asked the Lord, "What will become of us? Would we ever become one?"

At that moment I heard a mighty voice crack the empty silence of my heart etching a "Yes!" I became confident, and asked, "When?" "In time," was the reply.

MILLY
Oscar R.

I can remember my proudest moment like it was yesterday. It was the day I met Milly. I knew there was something special about her—a rare jewel. Everything fit her to perfection: big eyelashes accentuating gorgeous auburn eyes; a cute button nose casting shadows over ruby lips; ears, black hair, and neck framing the most beautiful face I have ever seen. If God has favorites, she must be his, having taken extra time to create this precious gem.

It was a gloomy spring day in 1996 when my family and I walked into the Chuck E. Cheese in Garden Grove, California. I don't remember if it was actually gloomy or it just felt that way because we had recently buried Danny, my thirteen-year-old brother. Whatever the reason for the murkiness of the day, it brightened the instant I laid eyes on Milly.

Seeing her sitting there, pretty and innocent, filled me with hope at a time when I felt my world was slipping away, that I was buried in uncertainty and confusion, and feared no one would find me in time. Then, there I was, looking at my glimmer of hope, shining bright as the sun.

At seventeen, I didn't know how to approach girls, feeling shy around any girl who wasn't my sister or mother. Past girlfriends had always initiated the relationship. Being an average Joe, I certainly wasn't attracting them with my looks; more likely is that I could offer a steady diet of drugs and alcohol, rendering them unable to make rational decisions. If viewed through sober eyes, I didn't stand a chance with a beautiful girl.

Despite my doubts, I could not let this chance pass. My cousin Manuel and I walked outside to his car to drink some courage. After three twelve ounce cans of Budweiser, I walked back into the place, slapping the furry mouse on the tail for good luck as I headed towards the pretty girl's table.

"Hi, I'm Casper, what's your name?" was my opening line. She smiled shyly with the innocence of a 15-year-old and said, "Hi Casper, I'm Milly." Whatever hesitation I felt up to that moment disappeared when I heard the sweetness in her voice. I had the best time of my teenage years that day, playing air hockey, laughing, and talking with God's Miracle, wishing I could suspend time and spend eternity in that moment. But I knew the natural law of time was impartial, ticking away as usual.

When it was time to say goodbye, I asked, "Will I ever see you again?" The uncertainty of life resumed. "I don't know," she replied, "but you can call me." The word "but" never sounded so good, making my heart leap with joy. I held her soft, warm hand as I said goodbye, desiring to hug and kiss her, but knew better, her mother's menacing stare watching my every move.

That spring day, God planted a seed in our hearts that would not blossom until more than a decade later. Thirteen years went by before I held Milly's hand again, in the prison visiting room. Every moment spent in love with her makes the long wait worthwhile. Love is patient.

CRAZY LADY
Patrick A.

Two debilitating strokes and four months of intense physical therapy transformed my grandmother's feet into four wheels, powered by daughter's legs, culminating in a prison house visit—both long awaited and rued. Cowering from the idea of her stroke, I shamefully feigned altruistic concern for my elder's ability to endure the rigors of travel in order to delay this day, this meeting. Now, selfishly averting eyes from wheelchair and hiding afore aged-frailty, I sought ignorance from how she now helplessly lists to one side.

For twenty-seven years, maternal love and a trusty Toyota Corolla toured California's juvenile and adult prison systems, dedicatedly touching Chinese-hewn walls of Folsom granite; creeping myopically through suffocating Corcoran fog; bravely skidding across icy Grapevine snow; and even, accidentally, invading Mexico, to embrace her undeserving head-to-toe tattooed grandson.

Our visits would normally begin with warm hugs, but noting she is unaccompanied, I hold her thin shoulder at arms length and shake her lovingly with admonishment, "You crazy lady, what are you doing driving all alone?!" Her smile leaves lipstick on my cheek.

Grandma is the hub of our family. Out-of-state relatives are obligated to ring her doorbell, and she is the person everyone turns to when in dire need.

As a child, I took her for granted; that is, until I found trouble. Then, the training wheels of a red Diamondback, her birthday gift to me, and my first two wheeler, would race to her embrace—a lioness ready to protect her pride. Refuge existed in her staunch belief that only blood punished blood, and to that blood, she, not even my mother, possessed sole right. I would be safe, no matter what my wrong, if I could peddle fast to sanctuary—Grandma's house.

With State vending machine sandwiches and pints of Dryer's Cherry Bomb ice cream, we would talk of everything, nothing, and the gossip in between. A prehistoric microwave, encrusted with the exploded contents of a cup of Hormel chili, remnants of some absent-minded visitor, substitutes for home cooking. Huddling around knee-high visiting tables isn't about the food, it's the company.

"So," I ask, "what's the latest?" Leaning close, in conspiracy, she rattles off the week's juiciest morsels. Saucy tid-bits top each bite of vending slop. The last courses served, she warns, "Don't say anything to anyone." Laughing, I look around the room of bald-headed convicts, thinking incredulously, who am I to tell? Maybe we get along because she entrusts me with family secrets, including her own.

In truth, I'm not sure how my grandmother and I became close. "Saint Patrick, Grandma's favorite," my sister scoffs in epithet. Perhaps being a lifer is akin to death, my sins buried behind prison walls, leaving only nostalgia to mythologize, to beatify.

I believe our unique relationship evolved from visiting time spent. To the rest of the family, Grandma could be abusively cold, demanding, and berating. But I am lucky to know her truly. I watch years drop from her shoulders when we embrace, becoming youthful, a jovial sprite with mischievous humor.

I am the only one who dares tell her off-color jokes and makes her laugh without offense. "What?!" I reply to my mother and sister's condemning eyes, "Are you afraid her virgin ears will burn?" Playfully my grandmother covers her own ears in mock horror and laughs even more. "How do you think you got here?" I badger, "Immaculate Conception?"

Perhaps I am irreverent, but it is who we are to each other, who we have become behind rows of razor wire. I wish my family knew Grandmother like I—her natural spontaneity and humor, her down to earthiness and overwhelming love for family. I am blessed to know my grandmother, beyond the sense simply that she lived to witness my birth, but rather, that she is my best friend—my constant.

I hate her stroke.

POPS
Brian L.

We had known each other from before, back when there was a real world. The connection between two grown men was our love for the same woman. To him, she was his soul mate, extra rib, other half; he called her his wife. To me, she was the source of life, she was the face of God on Earth; I called her mom.

After her passing, we were left with a heart shaped hole in our souls. Determined to keep him going, I decided to let him know I cared and that he was loved. I loved Mom enough to continue the relationship with him. Little did I know, he had decided to do the same.

Even though we shared no blood, we soon became father and son. Calls and letters each started with the same question, "How are you? Are you okay?" After a lifetime of not knowing the man that contributed to my creation, I had hardened my heart to keep out the pain of absence; my father's absence. Now, another man, with no allegiance owed to me, other than the strength of his word: he'd promised Mom that I would not be forgotten. And his word proved good. He became my father.

It seems bizarre that of all possible places and of all possible times, that it was here, and now, while I am doing a sentence equivalent to death, that I finally found him, the one I was lacking in my life.

I had come to know Ken as my dad. And it's my joy to call him my Pops.

THE YELLOW RIVER
Jojo D.

"G-52, visit!" The booming mic pulls a forlorn soul across the parched prison yard, as my parents await. A rare orchid, Mom's delicate petals sing love, bridging the barren gulf between Father and Son. Seeded by monsoons of an ancient wound, stone barriers crumble, loosing the mighty Yellow River upon my cheek; the great Yangtze upon his. The two distant rivers converge, flooding relief to our drought-stricken relationship. Emotional torrents bring closure—an oasis of tranquility.

"Son, I've been a prideful man, afraid of affection. But from this day, let nothing keep us apart," gushed the Yangtze.

"Together, let us be the strong Philippine Sea."

THE GOOD, THE BAD, AND THE UGLY
Julian V.

Julian: a name from ages past, originating with an ancient Greek god. He was the most powerful and best loved by all. My parents wanted me to have this name, which meant merciful, powerful, patience, and love, the bringer of a new day. I didn't like my name; in fact, I hated it. I wanted to be a "Butch" or a "Taco," maybe even a "Maddog."

In my youth, the "J" stood for Joker, for the ass I was. I was juvenile, judgmental, jaded and—the two that hurt most—junky and Judas to my God. "U" was for ugly, because of the way I felt inside. Uranus, because I always felt alien, from another planet. "L" connoted Lucifer, for the many times I played the Devil—a loser, lost, lonely, and lifeless. "I," because I lived in infamy. Ill-mannered, indulgent, inept, ignoramus. "A," an abomination: I was a cancer on society, pushing for anarchy, aggression, addiction, arrogance, abuse. "N," for nasty, naughty, neurotic. A nincompoop and nomad.

Today, I've learned to love myself and others. I'm in recovery and I am rebuilding myself. The "J" now stands for joy, for the smiles I enjoy putting on people's faces. And for justice, as I live awash with the blood of Jesus Christ. "U" is for upbeat and staying positive. Upkeep—maintaining and nourishing what I've learned, as I shine like the stars of Ursa-Major. "L" is for legacy, life, laughter, and love. "I," for insight into my mistakes. I illuminate a new path and inspire others to seek a better future. "A" is for Alleluja. I'm alive and saved, atoning for my wrongs. Abstention, academics, and adopting new behaviors—a new way of life! "N," for non-violence, a new start, new friends, and for establishing a nexus with my savior and creator. "Julian" is my name and what it means to me now.

TAKE NOTICE
Bradley F.

David said, "You should come check out this group I'm in". He didn't explain anymore, only that it was a self-help group. I walked into the chow hall somewhat closed off, not knowing what to expect. Thinking some free staff would be running the group, I was surprised to see an inmate up front. Instantly, my thoughts became jaded. How can another inmate help me?

Sensing I wasn't feeling it, Dave urged, "Just give it a chance". So I sat, listening, taking in the faces of the room—those I knew, liked, and disliked.

As the floor opened for anyone to share, he stepped to the front and introduced himself, "My name is Bernie." I knew of him. In Folsom, his name rang bells. Here, he was speaking on change, recovery, and allowing God to lead his life.

I sat up and took notice—my first day of CGA.

I FEEL YOU
Melvin P.

I cringe when someone I don't know says, "I feel you". Do you feel me? I mean really? How about that 1989 extension cord my heavy-handed father carved in to my legs? Can you feel the wincing pain or the bloody mess it left?

Do you feel all the little internal earthquakes of insecurity I suffer from? Do you feel the way I feel at the sound of the bass drum? The band Hate is music to my hears, so when I hear it I put on my dancing shoes. Do you?

America, land of the free, home of the brave. Whoever told you that is your enemy; you still feel me? Real gangsters and thugs don't wear ski masks and commit small robberies. They wear Brooks Brother suits, and work on Wall Street. Their sons play soccer, and daughters, the pep squad. Still feeling me?

If you could read my mind, I doubt you would still feel me. Everyday in prison, someone dies. When it's my cellmate or next door neighbor, I'm expected to publicly be sad and reminisce over the ice cream we shared on the handball court together that one time.

But all I really feel is jealousy, because they got out of prison before I did. Beware, lest anyone cheat you through empty deceit, according to the tradition of men. I'm trying to feel Jesus, but Satan keeps slapping my hands. I know people who can't afford to drive, so they use their feet. They get tired, but can't sit down, or Congress will come along and tax their seat. Meanwhile, Obama plays golf and everyone nods their heads, "Yes, we can" when he asks "Who feels me?"

Feelings are fickle and subject to change. When I'm high I feel shame, when I think back on my sentencing date I feel PAIN.

It feels like watching your life's dreams being baptized in acid rain. People like to talk, and rarely like to listen. That's why I don't share my story with people in prison. I keep my autobiography to myself, and if you call that selfish then, yeah, I'm guilty.

Now pass this around like a chain letter and see how many other people Feel Me.

LIFE
Shawn C.

The batter-dipped deep-fried cheese burns my tongue as the boardwalk comes alive. The breeze carries the aroma of saltiness and freshness, with a hint of honeysuckle.

The sea is in motion as the fishermen drop their lines. Boats on the horizon advance in slow motion. The sky's aflutter with birds, and planes, and parachutes of clouds.

Children fly kites as they enjoy the sun and construct sand castles. Parents lie in the sand, sunrays gently sizzling their skin, with hopes of becoming golden gods and goddesses by day's end. Chatter in the distance, I gaze through a window. Spotting a crystal sailboat with filled sails, I wish I was on it, hair blowing in the wind. I navigate the world and all its freedoms.

Raising my family, fear sets in as the bills come, praying I make it another month. Foreclosure stares me in the face. I sit in traffic, sweating, going to and from work. The things I endure to survive this freedom called life! The good and the bad of being free.

PART 8. LIGHTER FARE

All meaningful and lasting change starts first in your imagination and then works its way out. Imagination is more important than knowledge.

- Albert Einstein

DARK ROAST
Bernie F.

A strange aroma draws me from my dreams. Morning arrives and yawning begins. The day's plans creep slowly into consciousness. Slow, deliberate movements quicken, as the anticipation of the first cup propels clarity. Before tackling any task, I sit quietly enjoying that first cup of joe.

CHARLIE HUSTLE
Ralph P.

I have always been a baseball fan, but never rooted for the Cincinnati Reds. Pete Rose, AKA Charlie Hustle, however, has always been one of my favorites. His extraordinary accomplishments on the diamond are worthy of the Hall of Fame.

Charlie Hustle lived up to his nickname, even with the bookies. Unfortunately, this prevented him from reaching his goal. Barry Bonds, A-Rod, and Roger Clemens have been involved in Federal indictments and Senate judicial hearings about steroid use, yet they're eligible for the Hall of Fame ballot.

Charlie Hustle had a gambling addiction. In the late 1980's Mr. Rose was caught in a gambling scheme that prevented him from the greatest accolade an athlete can achieve—the Hall of Fame. Cooperstown is everything to a baseball giant. Major league baseball needs to allow Cincinnati's finest his due. In reality, Pete Rose did gamble. That's a fact. But he never once bet that the team he played for would lose. This is also a fact. To me, that is an awesome competitive spirit.

Nowadays you see baseball greats who have been involved in Federal indictments and Senate judicial hearings about steroid use, yet the public doesn't bat an eye. It's all good. Books are written—both negative and positive—and autobiographies; you name it!

Charlie Hustle lived up to his name because he was a hustler. No steroids have ever been mentioned in concert with his gigantic baseball name, yet, he's been punished the hardest. I don't get it. It is my own humble opinion that MLB Commissioner, Bud Selig, should permit Pete Rose to finally be inducted into baseball's Hall of Fame in Cooperstown, Ohio.

Will it happen? I don't know. But I'd bet on it.

SIREN'S CALL
Jojo D.

White sand crunches warm between my toes as turquoise waves fizz champagne upon island shores. Answering a siren's call, holding my breath, eyes open to watery greenhouse of coral reefs and swift darting neon fish. Releasing the ocean's soothing embrace, rivulets stream down from my sun-kissed chest, as I drift.

Tranquil seas recede for promise of plantain leaves topped with steaming rice and honey-walnut shrimp. Brown hammocks sway in the tropical breeze, dancing between lazy palms, green, coconut fronds finger painting marshmallows upon azure horizon. Paradise greets me with tiki torches and family.

Together, we dine.

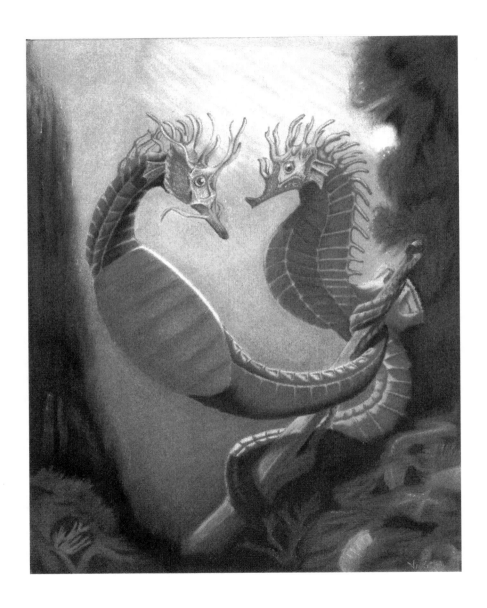

BAHAMIAN VACATION
Jorge R.

Apanoramic view of high palm trees, wild grass, gigantic leaves and other colorful plants. A beautiful blue ocean with high waves saying, "Come, play with me." A warm breeze blowing, opening my nostrils to the scent of fresh air and wild life.

Yellow, blue, and red were the colors of the sports cars parked on the sandy road, reminding me of my Columbian flag, giving my happy face a prideful smile. Walking on the hot sand tickled my toes.

Unbuttoning my white polo and removing my grey Levi's, leaving just my boxers, I ran toward the clear water, diving into its coldness, instantly refreshing my steaming body, leaving me breathless in the salty water.

Becoming part of its world I swam back and forth without a care. Diving in, I saw yet another world where playful fish greeted strangers in their water, caressing my legs as they swam, out of sight. Seaweed folklorically danced, exhibiting an underwater show I had never seen. Lobsters ran for cover, as shrimps played on the ocean floor.

Burning lungs forced me to surface. The waves rocked me back and forth as I floated, admiring the light blue sky and the colorful macaw birds that happily flew before my eyes.

Interrupted by the scream, "Praise the Lord," I realized I wasn't at the beach. The colorful Polynesian panorama depicted on the pastor's shirt had triggered my A.D.H.D., ushering me into another blissful daydream.

HOOD-A-WEEN
Angel R.

Hobo in da hood! Pops' ripped jeans held up wit a rope, shot-out boots that wreaked of dank leather, cigarette ashes smeared across face, a dead-end two-story old house covered in dried-up vines, the place every kid fears. Cracked windows, faded paint, century-old boards, peeling from decades of neglect. A hunch-backed old lady in black, who never smiles.

The house draws near. Double-dare, here I come! Creepy crawlers everywhere. Torn, worn curtains, patchy grass, yard ghosts. Dracula aside, eight other hobos chuckle and giggle, fingers pointing as they hold their breath, warped porch boards creaking beneath their steps.

A wrinkled face is spotted peeking. "Ahhhhh! Cheet-che sees me!" She cracks a sinister smile. Screen door squeaks open as she drags her dead leg behind her, reaching her wrinkled hand toward me. I strain to get a better look. "What the hell is dat?

Oh, Hell no!" I am stunned, unable to run. A dog's eyeball in her palm, she leans closer, grabs holdah my collar, and yanks me inside. Screen door slams shut. Screaming bloody murder, I can barely hear da little Dracula and other kids yelling, "Help! The Bruja's got Angel! The Bruja's got Angel!"

Inside da house, me and grandma collapse on the floor laughing so hard, tears run down our cheeks. "Best one yet, Nana! Didja see their faces!?" Gawd, how I love Halloween in da hood.

SMILE
Fred D.

Smile, I wish I could hold you tight
You verified on Mom's face, I did right
On faces, you shine so bright
But for you to get out, it's such a fight
Mona Lisa wore you great
I look forward to the day you're on every face
Flirting as you walk by
Sealed on, when loved ones die
A constant friend you've always been
carried me through thick and thin
it's been a gift, at no cost
caused me to see gain in the midst of loss
my healer of much pain
a helper that many restrain
Some say you're a frown upside down
Or what children see on a clown
Every child has a smile
Then, with age, it gets lost somehow
So when my sunny days are dimmed by clouds
I pray for the brightness of at least one smile.

PILLOW TALK

Johnny S.

Solitary confinement has finally taken it's toll upon my weary, lonely soul. But in the dark pit of despair, where hate multiplies like cancerous cells, I stumbled upon one of prison life's rare gems—a "true friend"—one who does not judge, understanding we are imperfect men; a friend who does not condemn, but forgives, allowing me space to vent or whisper sweet nothings.

In the heat of the night, body glistening with sweat, I shivered and shuddered, as an angry beast feasted on my soul, leaving my mind clouded with a hate I could not control. But in my arms, night after night, never uttering a word of my darkest secrets, absorbing my fears and pain through the sweat and silent tears, the reassuring softness of my faithful and loyal friend pressed against my face.

The years passed slowly for my friend and me, yet none ever heard a complaint or cross word. Now tattered and torn, stained and worn, time has begun to take its toll. Upon my soft pillow, till sweet dreams end—my ever-faithful friend.

PART 9. BREAKING FREE

When I write, I am free.

- Melvin P., writer (RJD)

BREAKING DOWN THE WALLS
Robert G.

"Robert, you're up." Hearing that, my heart starts racing. Pushing back the chair, I stand and stroll to the podium. It's my time to shine, literally, as I share what I have written for class.

I begin reading, looking up occasionally making eye contact. I feel the stares of all in the room beaming back at me, the heat in my body rises, and sweat begins to glisten on my forehead. The saliva in my mouth dries up, making it hard for me to speak. Feeling like I'm standing in an oven, my skin becomes shiny with moisture, as my nerves boil.

I've been so nervous that I've even skipped a whole paragraph when reading to the group. Leaving the podium that day I wondered, "What the heck is wrong with me?"

I am a man who has lived more than half my life around the most dangerous men in California without being nervous, yet I become frightened when reading to a small group of people in a class?

I know it is not because I am weak. It takes courage to open up and reveal pain from childhood abuse, as well the shame and guilt I feel from disgracing myself about the cowardly sins I've committed against countless victims.

Breaking down the walls, making myself vulnerable by exposing my insecurities through writing, and sharing them for the first time in my life, has given me the opportunity to finally unload them, to forgive, to heal, and to grow more than I have ever imagined possible.

AN EMOTIONAL CHAIN
Oscar M.

Today we had our first meeting. Interesting as it may have been, we were assigned homework. TOPIC: My Insecurities. For some strange reason, this question seems to punch me right in the face. Why do I feel so reluctant? I am not sure. Could it be that I might expose more than I should? Will I reveal my soft underbelly, thus arming potential enemies?

The "big me" confidently says I have no insecurities. I repeat this over and over, as if to reassure myself. In the process, I try to re-establish confidence and self-worth. However, the little me, the one who wants change and to build upon the remaining ashes of my past, knows that I must establish a firm foundation—one built around honesty, trust, and integrity.

I realize my insecurities relate closely to my fear—a paralyzing type of fear. I am insecure because I fear that I might not fit in. Fit into what? Fit in as a functioning and contributing member of society.

I tremble with the haunting doubt that I may not be smart enough, that I may not be well-liked. I chill at the thought of exposing certain parts of my past. Will the positive image I have begun to create for myself shatter under scrutiny?

I am fearful at the prospect of fully trusting people! I am confident, sure, but mostly about my uncertainty! Will the future extend a compassionate hand? Must I find the confidence to describe my own worth—or will that strike others as boastful self-promotion? Or can I just *be* me—the *new* me?

LIFE'S LESSON
Cesar L.

Bumps and bruises abound. Choosing one over another would be doing one of life's lesson an injustice, for each is well deserving of its tale.

I will share an experience that made this grown man cry. Since the beginning of this wonder of words, I began to realize just how many opportunities we have collectively missed. I've felt your pain; I've heard your stories of loss, and I've shared your joy as you found direction within this great maze of words to produce some beautiful works. Each man has let shine part of his humanity, warming the soul with hope that all is not lost.

I've seen old grizzled faces crack the tough-guy exteriors, and young timid faces grow confident, even bold, as they shared words of encouragement. So many opportunities to live, laugh, love, hope, and grow makes this grown man cry tears of joy.

Thank you!

TOMORROW IS TODAY
Manuel B.

I am sitting on my bunk, hesitant to pick up my pen because I know why I must. This is my last essay for Creative Writing class. It went by too damn fast.

Reminds me of that summer fling you have when you were in junior high. One minute you're on top of the world and the next, fun's over. The topic we were supposed to write about is "tomorrow." Tomorrow is today, as I'm stand here at this podium, looking out at each and every one of you. I hope you can all see my gratitude beaming out from my tattooed eyelids. I thank each and every one of you for all of your time and your help. I hate good-byes.

Tomorrow is today and yesterday already feels a million miles away. Twenty-four hours from now, when the sun goes to bed and the moon comes out to play, I'm going to remember the good times I had— yesterday, today, and for a million tomorrows.

SUCCESS AT LAST
Jojo D.

"**S**on, your father and I are so proud of you. We love you." Her voice cracked with emotion! Over the phone, I could hardly understand anything they said. All I heard was that I made them proud, as my heart erupted with joy. I never imagined my work being covered by the *Union-Tribune* and blasted across the internet into my parent's home, delivering untold happiness.

Photos were taken while a professional writer imparted to our class the finer points of polished speech (That is what he told us writing was like.) Tiko drums beat wildly in my chest, fear and excitement swirling with the unexpected. To my surprise, he referred to me by my first name, and my anxiety melted away. John's rural Kansas energy lent genteel persuasion to his vicious critique that left me hungering for more.

After class, I returned to my cell with an overpowering urge to write. I found my voice in paper expression; freedom pulsed from my pen like an Energizer Bunny. I wrote all night.

All my life I have burdened my family, broken hearts, and grieved their souls, but writing with a group of bravely non-judgmental students has given me a positive purpose. My proudest moment—the moment I made my parents proud.

PICK AND SHOVEL
Oscar M.

Our class on creative writing is coming to a close. Sarah motivated me to speak. She mentioned my letter, which impacted her. The topic was love and happiness. I wrote mine on domestic violence and my deep regret of being a stupid, macho abuser. She cried last week. She personally related to the pain. In fact, she is still waiting for an apology from that someone.

The Sergeant walked in while the people were still speaking. His presence seemed to make the atmosphere tighten. I noticed that people started to cross their arms, making me withdraw as well. I started to think, "I'll share my feelings with the class only after custody leaves." To my surprise, not only did he not leave, he got involved!

Apparently inspired by the level of emotion in the room, he jumped in. I remember what happened: Someone thanked the sponsors and custody for allowing this unique class to happen, since it seemed totally out of character for the prison. The sergeant began to share his own perspective on prison, on programs, and on staff and inmate relationships. He spoke about his humble beginnings as a state employee. He started off as a maintenance man before becoming a correctional officer, then a sergeant. He had worked with inmates on a close, human level.

This seemed to ease the grip I had on my emotions. A couple of other persons spoke. Then, I felt compelled. I started off by acknowledging Sarah's genuine, "I thank you for sharing your letter with the class." I apologized for making her cry, since my intentions were simply to bring healing between my family and me. I pray that it will do the same for others.

What I got out of this class was truly incredible. I broke through many barriers. I have to admit, when it came down to it, that I hated writing. I was illiterate when I came to prison. How I struggled! Looking for words in the dictionary became an unwelcome task. Often, I couldn't even find the word I was trying to spell.

My negative academic experiences had made me view myself as a pick and shovel man, preferring the challenge of digging a hole to the mental strain of writing. I had to work harder, to compensate for my weak academic skills. I had, long ago, been traumatized by the debilitating feeling of failure. This experience has put layer upon layer of confidence on me. I surprised myself. I now like to write.

I will miss the students. They became very special people. I really enjoyed seeing them every Wednesday. At first, I was skeptical. How would this all unravel? All I knew is that they made me nervous. I was supposed to open up to them—these strangers? It was a hurdle I had to overcome.

I was saddened to discover that I was making them feel nervous, as well. It was neat to see that, in the end, we were all simply people. As the weeks passed we relaxed and looked forward to the common goal. Writing bridged our distinct communities!

I never imagined that I would be seen as having writing talent. My confidence blossomed. I'm happy with my progress. And I am a better person.

EVERYTHING AND NOTHING
Manuel B.

It's amazing how quickly time flies. To a man serving time in prison, it can be a friend or enemy. Or it can be both. It is my friend because I got to spend time with some wonderful people who taught me much. They taught me to harness the power of words and to tame frustration with punctuation. They taught me confidence in my storytelling abilities—and myself.

But time is also my enemy, because our time has run out in this class and has ended our time together. It passed us by like a sprinter past an injured competitor.

I am forever grateful to everyone who took their time to teach us and to show us patience when we hit obstacles. If you ask what this experience means to me, it means everything to me. Nothing could ever make me forget how special it was.

FOUND
Oscar R.

Learning to explore the deepest regions of my mind, heart, and soul has given me a new-found freedom. I have a voice in the silent movement of a thundering BIC ballpoint pen. "We are all writers," echoes in my mind, recalling what we were told the first week of what turned into a life–changing experience. I had my doubts about that statement, but as my class comes to an end, I understand the conviction in John Brown's voice. I uncovered more than the writer in me. I found the husband, the father, the thirty-three-year-old boy, the attentive listener who learned to respect a reader's time, and, perhaps most importantly, a grateful human being.

EMOTIONS
Jojo D.

Writing brought peace to my life, enabling my crippled conscience to release waves of thorns and daggers wedged deep in my heart. Whirlwinds of pain and joy flowed through a fine tipped point onto a blue-lined canvas.

I was stripped naked, vulnerable, and scared, but with the Spirit of Tigers, courage engulfed me, lending me the strength to share my deepest emotions with my father.

With the help of college professors, students, and inmates, a writer was born and through this experience, pride, joy, and—most of all—healing.

LORI B. SUTTON & L. PAUL SUTTON, eds.

MATT.
26:14-16
JOHN
13:38

BY
Sal 2013

SINNERS
L. Paul Sutton ©2012

We thought we surely knew
What's good and bad, and true
But study will dispel
Those lessons learned so well

Indeed, they were so clear--
Those truths that we held dear
So hard, as days grow long,
To gather we were wrong

Reality is not
As simple as we thought
The public do not know
The truth behind the show

The media declared
That we should all be scared
And hate the souls who crawl
Behind the prison wall

Fists raised above our head,
We're quick to damn and dread
Those buried in that lair--
Condemned to perish there

This beaten path we tread
From fiction we have read
Most versions fail to tell
That prison life is hell

Most stories never said
That prison's dark and red
And souls who try too hard
Die quickly on the yard

These teachings never told
How youth turns rarely old
And hearts, afraid to beat,
Are ruptured in defeat

The masks men use to sell
Indifference to their hell
Protect them from the glare
Of those who do not care

Truth, too, dies in the yard
For honesty's too hard
A mask, the devil's hood,
Hides any hint of good

Those convicts, to be sure
Deservedly endure
Good measure of our scorn
For evil they have borne

"Impossible to see
They're anything like me"
Becomes our trite refrain
To justify the pain

But faces behind bars
Are not so unlike ours
Where hopes turn quick to sighs
Dreams murdered by their lies

They live in senseless strife
This irony of life
Hate spews with every breath
Lest decency bring death

I wonder now aloud
To patrons who are proud
To banish to such graves
This lot of kindred knaves

Did they who lie within
Commit the greater sin?
Or we, who cast their fate
To graveyards groomed with hate.

ABOUT THE EDITORS

Paul Sutton's path into the world of corrections meandered unpredictably from the high plains of Kansas through the storied yards of Attica, San Quentin, Folsom, and notorious Pelican Bay.

Spending his formative years in middle America, Sutton graduated summa cum laude from the University of Kansas with a double major in political science and history in the days of the Viet Nam riots and the Kent State tragedy. With a fellowship to study criminal justice at the State University of New York in Albany, Sutton earned a PhD five years later, in 1975, in the aftermath of one of American's greatest social and political upheavals. *Serpico, Cool Hand Luke, Brubaker, and Titticut Follies* delivered the message of systemic corruption and ineptitude in the American justice system every bit as powerfully as did the scholarly accounts by the President's Crime Commission (the voluminous *Challenge of Crime in a Free Society*) and the fathers of criminological theory and progressive reformers like Norval Morris, who filled the Albany curricula.

In graduate school, Sutton volunteered with the Rockefeller Commission, appointed to investigate the Attica prison riot; worked as the first intern for the Federal Bureau of Prisons in Petersburg Federal Reformatory; and participated in a number of national-scope research projects at the Hindelang Research Center in Albany. There, his work included the conceptualization and creation of the *Sourcebook of Criminal Justice Statistics*; a massive feasibility study on sentencing guidelines; studies of juvenile delinquency; a national training program for state crime planners about policy applications of the National Crime Victimization Survey data; and studies on crime victims, the victimization process, and state crime victim compensation programs.

After Albany, Sutton joined the sociology faculty at the University of New Mexico as an assistant professor. While there, a tour of the Penitentiary of New Mexico with his criminology class renewed his focus on corrections and launched what was to become a secondary career in documentary filmmaking. He co-produced *Doing Time* to expose the public to critical, but little understood, realities about incarceration, and the men and women who live and work behind the walls. His first feature prison documentary, *Doing Time* was broadcast around the world, received three Emmy Awards, and garnered numerous film festival laurels.

Weeks after *Doing Time* was first broadcast, the Penitentiary of New Mexico erupted in the bloodiest prison riot in American history. Sutton returned to that ill-fated prison to reprise the events of the intervening decade in his second Emmy-winning documentary— *Doing Time: Ten Years Later.*

After *Doing Time*, Sutton returned to the world of quantitative and qualitative analysis at the National Center for State Courts, exploring the link between learning disabilities and juvenile delinquency; sentencing guidelines; and the operation of the Fourth Amendment (search and seizure) across the U.S. The research into the last of these was cited in the U.S. Supreme Court's seminal decision in *U.S. v. Leon*, which created the "good faith" exception to the exclusionary rule.

Subsequently, Sutton was appointed coordinator of the criminal justice program in the School of Public Affairs at San Diego State University. There, in 1983, he created the California PrisonTour, a weeklong, 1500-mile charter bus excursion through a variety of correctional programs and institutions across California.

As director of that program, for the next 30-plus years, Sutton escorted nearly 3,000 criminal justice majors from SDSU and other schools on 113 weeklong excursions through nearly two dozen prison sites, including Folsom, San Quentin, Pelican Bay, Soledad, and the Delancey Street Foundation in San Francisco. During that time, he and his wife, Lori, got to know hundreds of prison officials, staff, and prisoners—intimately. That experience—and those acquaintances—formed the basis of their next five prison documentaries, as well as the writing program they created at RJD prison in San Diego, which gave rise to this volume.

To introduce the public to many of the little known realities of incarceration, the Suttons documented most of their forays into prison with the production of feature documentaries. *Prison Through Tomorrow's Eyes* chronicled the events of one of those weeklong excursions through prisons, as students spoke with prisoners and staff in eight different prisons all over the state. *The Legend of Alfredo Santos* tells the story of the famed prison artist who painted the history of California on the massive dining room walls of San Quentin. *POOCH* recounts the selfless efforts of prisoners at RJD who train service animals for use by disabled veterans and autistic children. *Badass* tracks the career of a retired San Quentin Sergeant who spent nearly 30 years behind the walls of San Quentin. And, finally, *Straight from the Pen* documents the innovative writing class that spawned this volume, a class that grew out of PrisonTour students' challenge to Sutton to do something more constructive, more impactful, something "more" than "simply" running the tours.

Lori Sutton worked for nearly two decades in local news in San Diego after studying telecommunications and film at SDSU. She assisted with the PrisonTours for the last half of that program's 33-year span, meeting and working with staff and prisoners all over the state. She developed powerful working personal relationships inside prisons, quite independently of Paul's work on the same projects.

Over the course of her years working with the men and women on the inside, she married her technical telecommunications skills with her passion to reform what she had witnessed in the prison world. Accordingly, Lori coordinated many of Paul's projects inside, photographed most of the video footage documenting our writing, and did yeoman's work teaching, supervising, and grading the prisoners' writings for class after class. Finally, the Alfredo Santos and POOCH documentaries are largely products of her imagination and work.